THE PEOPLE YOU MEET IN HELL

A TROUBLING ALMANAC OF THE
VERY WORST HUMANS IN HISTORY

THE
PEOPLE
YOU MEET
IN HELL

BRIAN BOONE   ILLUSTRATIONS BY PIPI SPOSITO

CASTLE POINT BOOKS
NEW YORK

www.castlepointbooks.com

The Castle Point Books trademark is owned by Castle Point Publishing, LLC.
Castle Point books are published and distributed by St. Martin's Publishing Group.

ISBN 978-1-250-28779-3 (trade paperback)
ISBN 978-1-250-28818-9 (ebook)

Edited by Jennifer Calvert
Design by Joanna Williams

Our books may be purchased in bulk for promotional, educational, or business use.
Please contact your local bookseller or the Macmillan Corporate and Premium Sales
Department at 1-800-221-7945, extension 5442, or by email at
MacmillanSpecialMarkets@macmillan.com.

First Edition: 2023

10 9 8 7 6 5 4 3 2 1

CONTENTS

A Special Place
IN HELL

Human beings contain multitudes. Depending on factors like stress, hunger, and lack of morning coffee—and whether or not they're in possession of a cold, dead heart—the average individual may be capable of breathtaking moments of kindness or haunting acts of wickedness. And we're not just talking about leaving a shopping cart in the middle of a parking lot (although that is pretty awful). We're talking about the kind of depravity that makes aliens lock their spaceship doors when they pass this crazy planet of ours. Hey, nobody's perfect! We're all dealing with stuff, and we all handle it in different ways. So we shouldn't judge, right?

Nah. We should judge. And judge we shall, because some humans are the absolute worst, and they deserve to be called out as such. Here, then, is *The People You Meet in Hell: A Troubling Almanac of the Worst Humans in History.* Think of this book as the Human Being Hall of Fame . . . if the voting committee were comprised entirely of dictators, bigots, serial killers, and politicians. And let's not forget the middle managers, gym teachers, and Karens of the world (all of whom made it in, by the way; congrats all around!). You'll find their tales of woe and self-importance interspersed with those of the most wretched among us—just to keep things light. Evil is on a spectrum, and this book runs the gamut.

We're not the only ones doing the judging in this waggish tome of terribleness. Each profile in *The People You Meet in Hell* includes star ratings and orders for individualized punishments straight from the big guy himself—a tofu-heavy diet for Jeffrey Dahmer, a citizenry of angsty teen demons for Ivan the Terrible, and a karmic flavor explosion for Jim Jones are just the start. Satan has one hell of a sense of humor. And it's just so satisfying to imagine these toxic narcissists and cartoon-villain wannabes paying for making the world a significantly worse place. So read on—and be glad you're not among them!

POWERFULLY
WICKED

CALIGULA

★★★☆☆
for Debauchery

In much the same way that all nineteenth-century presidents seemed to have huge mustaches, pretty much all of the ancient Roman emperors were psychopaths bent on world domination. But surely they couldn't *all* have been so deplorable. It's just that Caligula (aka Gaius Julius Caesar Augustus Germanicus) was so deplorable that his reputation spilled over and stained those of his predecessors and successors like beer at a frat party. Caligula was so gross that the customary big British biopic about him was basically porn.

A few months into his four-year reign (37 to 41 CE), Caligula announced that he was a god and thus infallible and free from consequence. He nearly bankrupted Rome for vanity projects, like forming a three-mile bridge out of merchant ships just so he could ride his horse on it while wearing a golden cape. Then he staged a very real and very expensive war with the god Neptune, ordering troops to whip the ocean and steal seashells as plunder. He also fed spectators to the lions on days that the gladiator games were low on prisoners to torture. And, adding insult to degenerate injury, he tried to appoint his favorite horse, Incitatus, to the Roman consulate. Caligula finally met his end when he was stabbed thirty times by his political allies. Who could have seen that coming?

Re: Eternal Damnation

Caligula gets to spend eternity with the horse he loved so much—but now the horse loves him back, and there's no escaping his amorous advances.

—Satan

NERO

★★★★★
for Stoking All the Fires

"WHAT AN ARTIST DIES IN ME!"

—THE HUMBLE MUSICIAN'S LAST WORDS

Nero probably didn't play his fiddle (or even a more historically accurate lyre) while Rome burned in a massive fire in 64 CE, but it's such an apt metaphor for this dumpster fire of a destructive and careless human being that it endured throughout history. Here's what actually did happen: Nero took control of the Roman Empire at sixteen—an age when most boys can barely control their emotions, let alone a quarter of the known world. His mother tried to turn him into her political puppet, but Nero was no mama's boy (although some accounts of their relationship have real *Game of Thrones* vibes). So the calculating matriarch tried to install his stepbrother, Britannicus, in his place. Instead, Nero had them both killed. The consummate family man then killed his mistress-turned-wife Poppaea by kicking her in her pregnant belly. (Considering that Nero reportedly ordered his first wife banished, bound, cut, suffocated, and beheaded, Poppaea probably should have swiped left.)

Nero may not have actually started the melee that saw Rome burn, but he did build his extravagant palace on its smoldering ruins. And that didn't sit well with his displaced and destitute constituents, who eventually ran their tone-deaf emperor out of town and replaced him. With no more murders or musical performances left to live for, Nero took one final life in exile: his own.

Re: Eternal Damnation

This one's almost too easy: Nero burns while gleeful Romans play fiddles around him. And if he takes the occasional Roman sandal to the gut, so be it.

—Satan

THE PEOPLE YOU MEET IN HELL

THEODOSIUS I

for Unsportsmanlike Conduct

Historically speaking, emperor Theodosius I was best known for harshing everyone's vibe. One of the first Christian emperors in the waning days of the Roman Empire, he outlawed the polytheism practiced by pretty much everyone, and with deadly consequences for offenses. But the emperor's piousness wasn't his worst quality. He threw a popular chariot racer in a prison dungeon when he was suspected of being a homosexual . . . in ancient Rome, where the lines of human sexuality were fairly blurry. When protests and riots erupted over the athlete's imprisonment, Theodosius pacified the crowd by saying he'd release the athlete and let him race the next day. It was a trap. Theodosius' soldiers killed all 7,000 people who arrived at the stadium to watch the race.

In light of this abominable act of casual mass slaughter, whatever good things Theodosius may have done while emperor have been relegated to footnotes. Building roads or erecting buildings doesn't seem to matter to historians when it's overshadowed by a despicable act of petty revenge with a body count. But it's worth mentioning that the buzzkill also put an end to the beloved Olympics because they were tainted by the old gods. Fun guy.

Re: Eternal Damnation

When he's not with me, Theodosius the Not-So-Great gets to wait hand-and-foot on all the gods, named and unnamed, at our weekly dinner parties. Serving Bacchus should be especially fun for him.

xPluto

ATTILA THE HUN

for Diplomacy

> "TRAMPLE THE WEAK.
> HURDLE THE DEAD."
>
> —ATTILA THE HUN,
> OBVIOUS EMPATH

If everything you know about the Huns comes from Disney's *Mulan*, you're still pretty well informed. In the fifth century CE, the nomadic Huns dominated Central Asia and Europe, riding around from village to village, plundering and wreaking havoc. They were led in their wanderings by two warrior brothers, Attila and Bleda, for more than a decade. But Huns are gonna Hun. When Attila got tired of the whole coleader thing, he murdered his dear old bro.

From that point on, Attila really built up the reputation of the Huns as a marauding force of death and chaos. He led the brutal charge to acquire most of the eastern Roman Empire. But Attila had a softer side, too, which he used to collect large fees from villages and countries in exchange for negotiating alliances with other rulers in a Mafia-style protection racket. Of course, he'd usually pillage everything and kill everyone anyway. So, maybe not so soft. After running rampant through present-day Russia, Ukraine, Germany, and the Balkans and killing tens of thousands of people, Attila suffered an equally impressive death: choking on his own nosebleed, in his sleep, on his wedding night.

Re: Eternal Damnation

The so-called Scourge of God gets the usual violent torture but with a special soundtrack: the one and only album by Attila, a 1960s psychedelic metal band fronted by Billy Joel, coincidentally cited as the worst rock album ever made.

–Satan

GENGHIS KHAN (TEMÜJIN)

★★★★★
for General Slaughter

Like most people, and leaders especially, Genghis Khan (born Temüjin) contained multitudes. An objectively great and effective leader, Temüjin rose up from anonymity in the twelfth and thirteenth centuries to unite the various nomadic tribes of Mongolia into one militaristic, super-nomadic society. He conquered most of China and Central Asia, building an empire roughly the size of Africa and earning the title Genghis Khan (aka "Universal Ruler"). His descendants occupied lands as far west as Poland and as far east as Korea.

Not only was Genghis Khan the G.O.A.T. of collecting territory, he was also a kind and just ruler—as long as you loved and supported him unconditionally, that is. He conquered and united by force. And if you showed any resistance, he and his mob wouldn't so much negotiate with you as slaughter you on sight. If you want to make an omelet, you have to break a few eggs, right? Well, Khan broke about 40 million of them, which is objectively a lot—and was also about 10 percent of the entire world population back then. But he did create the first continental postal system, so . . . not all bad?

Re: Eternal Damnation

Genghis gets to be the official tour guide of Hell! He'll perform like a Disney cast member for hordes of demons and the newly damned. And the only thing he gets to conquer is his customer service voice.

–Satan

THE PEOPLE YOU MEET IN HELL

TIMUR (TAMERLANE)

for Imitating Greatness

> "... KNOW THAT THREE THINGS GO BEFORE ME, DEVASTATION, BARRENNESS, AND PESTILENCE ..."
> —TIMUR, CORRECTLY IDENTIFYING HIMSELF AS A PLAGUE

Every professional has a hero, someone they look up to and try to emulate—even conquerors who seemingly only want to acquire land so they can kill however many thousands of people already live on it. For Middle Eastern warlord Timur in the late 1300s, that hero was Genghis Khan. He wanted to be that ruthless occupier the way Dawson Leery wanted to be the next Steven Spielberg. He even joined Khan's son Chagatai's military campaign to get a whiff of that murderous infamy.

Timur amassed armies who were on board with his vision for world domination (or, maybe, who were just terrified of being on the other side). Together, they invaded what's now India, Pakistan, and Iraq, and killed pretty much everyone they encountered. He even killed people for being too tolerant of other people (the monsters!). All in all, Timur was responsible for the deaths of 17 million people—that's 5 percent of the entire world population at the time. His legacy is plenty evil to land him a special place in Hell, but he never did play at Genghis Khan's level. It's no coincidence that "Tamerlane"—the Persians' salty nickname for him, which translates to "Timur the Lame"—has stuck for the last six centuries or so. Close, but no cigar, buddy!

Re: Eternal Damnation

Since Timur likes imitations so much, he gets to spend eternity stuck in Chuckles, Hell's comedy club, where he'll be subjected to hacky 1980s comedians doing impressions of him.

—Satan

Vlad the Impaler

★★★★☆
for Sticking and Poking

You've got to be pretty evil to inspire the creation of a mythical bloodsucking monster, even if that monster later inspires goofy cartoons, Muppets, and cringey teen romances. Still something of a folk hero in Romania, Vlad Dracula (yes, that's where the name comes from—zero creativity points for Bram Stoker) ruled over the region of Wallachia for a couple months in 1448 and again from 1456 to 1476. He wasn't technically a count, but he was an indiscriminate murderer with an inexplicable taste for human blood—metaphorically speaking.

Vlad brutally dispatched anyone who so much as mildly wronged him or his kingdom, killing more than 80,000 people according to historians. OK, sure, leaders have to kill invading hordes and enemies all the time. But Vlad seemed to enjoy that part of the job more than most, torturing adversaries in creative and brutal ways. When diplomats refused to remove their hats for religious reasons, he had the hats nailed to their skulls. And, of course, he earned his unimaginative but catchy nickname by running poles through his enemies and displaying their heads on stakes outside his castle as a warning not to do anything Vlad doesn't like. Karmically, when the Ottomans finally killed him in battle, they took his head as a trophy.

Re: Eternal Damnation

You know that chair in the corner of every bedroom that serves as a dumping ground for not-quite-clean laundry? Impale Vlad's fully conscious head and body on different pikes by Hell's laundry room. He's that chair now.

–Satan

POPE ALEXANDER VI

for Bad Poping

Today, the Pope is merely the leader of the billion-strong Roman Catholic Church. But as most European countries adopted Catholicism as their state religion, and the Church itself controlled vast swaths of land, popes were once more like statesmen. At times, you might even have called them *dictators*. And it's in this era when Pope Alexander VI ruled.

Born Rodrigo Borgia, Pope Alexander VI was no moral pillar for the world or representative of Christ on Earth. First of all, celibacy was not his thing; this guy was like the fifteenth-century Nick Cannon, fathering kids with mistresses left and right. And with all the vainglorious swagger of a Roman emperor or a blindly power-mad and amoral Shakespearean king, Borgia bribed the papal electors with his vast family wealth to become the most powerful man on the planet. Then he appointed his unqualified offspring to power (literally the reason the celibacy rule existed in the first place) and killed off rival church officials so he could steal their property (arguably worse than bedding women). And his legacy of murderous tyranny didn't end with him. Bolstered by Daddy's nepotism and ruthlessness, Cesare and Lucrezia Borgia became notoriously evil in their own right. Talk about role models!

Re: Eternal Damnation

An iconic holy man would surely enjoy attending a classic Catholic Mass in Latin, surrounded by his fellow clergymen. But while most sermons only feel endless, this one actually is.

—Satan

Autocorrect Inventors

★★★☆☆
for Uselessness

The people who foist technology upon the world claim that it's going to make life easier, that it will save time and complete mundane tasks so we can get to the fun stuff that much quicker, or that it will get the simple, necessary tasks out of the way. And sometimes it does. Computers, for example—solid invention. They make things smoother by and large, simplifying processes, allowing people to work from anywhere, and giving us a world of information at our fingertips. (Whether or not we use it well is on us.) But autocorrect, the now-native software that plagues every smartphone on the planet, is a technological albatross. Thanks so much, person who arrogantly decided that word recognition software should be as prudish and presumptuous as they were. No, no, no, we know what you really meant to say. Here, we'll just say it for you. Who asked them to edit our texts in the first place? And then they have the audacity to be wrong more often than not. This life-changing service doesn't save much labor when you have to retype the word you wanted to say three or four times. Its only redeeming quality is the abundance of hilarious memes and screengrabs its failures have spawned. In short, autocorrect and its arrogant inventors really ducking sock.

> **Re: Eternal Damnation**
>
> If they can text me a simple note asking to be released from Hell, they're free to go. But autocorrect knows they really want to stay, and there's no "undo" option, so that's going to be tricky.
>
> —Satan

IVAN THE TERRIBLE

for Sheer Terribleness

> "BESIDE [IVAN THE TERRIBLE],
> NERO WAS MILD."
>
> —E. H. GOMBRICH, STATING THE OBVIOUS

Ivan's official historical epithet is literally "terrible," so this one's clearly a no-brainer. Otherwise known as Ivan IV Vasilyevich, Ivan was the grand prince of Moscow in the sixteenth century. Early in his reign as the first crowned czar of Russia, he centralized the Russian state and made popular reforms. Not too terrible so far, right? But, like a mall cop on a motorized scooter, the power went to this paranoid tyrant's head.

Ivan became increasingly unhinged. Every political machination he undertook involved massive death tolls. He had his advisers killed so he could have all the power to himself. He started a bloody war throughout Eastern Europe that lasted twenty-five years. And he had Russia's noble class tortured and killed in the most horrific ways imaginable—we're talking boiled alive, roasted over a spit, or drawn and quartered.

Ivan was just as terrible in his personal life. During one of his fits of rage, he beat his eldest son's pregnant wife until she miscarried. Then he murdered that son for confronting him about it, leaving his younger son to inherit the throne. He, in turn, ended the family's dynasty by dying childless, kicking off the aptly named Time of Troubles. Not big on forethought, this guy.

Re: Eternal Damnation

Ivan the Power Hungry can give all the orders he wants down here, but the angsty teenage demons who surround him will drive him mad by ignoring every word he says. He better learn how to make pizza rolls!

–Satan

THE PEOPLE YOU MEET IN HELL

OLIVER CROMWELL

for Profiling

> "HE HAS LEFT US WITH LITTLE MORE
> THAN A NAME TO CURSE."
>
> —JOHN MILTON, LOYAL FRIEND

Oliver Cromwell was a complicated guy. Did he help modernize European politics away from power-mad monarchs in the seventeenth century with a parliamentary, democratic-based form of government? Sure. And when he was put in charge, did he rule England with reason and sense? Depends on who you ask. General opinion of Cromwell was pretty high in those days if you happened to be English. If you were Irish, didn't enjoy being spied on, liked having a free press, or had a distaste for slaughter, not so much.

Cromwell was hired by the British government to put the kibosh on any gains for Irish independence during the Rebellion of 1641, which aimed to evict the Irish and their military. Under his direction, Cromwell's New Model Army (as in Elvis Costello's "Oliver's Army") arrived in Drogheda and pretty much killed everyone with Irish blood. Dissenters, British supporters, Protestants, Catholics—it didn't matter to him. If you were Irish, you were dead. He used spies to tamp down dissent and the government to ban any books or newspapers that didn't paint him in a good light, which may be why history is mixed on whether he's a hero or a tyrant. But here he is in Hell, so that should clear things up!

Re: Eternal Damnation

Cromwell's soul will inhabit—and feel every tap, scrape, and stomp made on—a stage used by a world-class Irish step-dancing troupe.

–Satan

Your Obnoxious Boss

★ ★ ★ ☆ ☆

on His Performance Review

How did this guy make it to middle management? With his permanent sneer, ugly tie, and zero people skills, how did someone so *meh* make it out of kindergarten? It's baffling and maddening and only made worse by the fact that this human sweater vest makes quadruple your salary. Does he get a bonus for being as annoying as possible? He must. That would explain the frequent vacations to Anywhere But Here.

You do his work for him, take the fall for all his bad ideas, and keep the company in the black by managing around him. What does he do? He cuts out early in his Maserati, but not before piling more work on your desk while standing too close and cracking an off-color joke. More offensive than any sexist snipe is his coffee breath. But worst of all is the fact that this dude actually believes his skills got him to where he is, and not the heady combination of nepotism and beer-soaked networking. This freaking guy.

Re: Eternal Damnation

It's time for Boss Man to get a taste of his own micromanaging. Stuck in a cubicle all day doing mind-numbing work, he's free to go at 4:59—*if* he can navigate his way out of the maze of cubicles and slip past the CEO of Useless Tasks. Spoiler: he never will.

—Satan

ANDREW JACKSON

★★★★☆
for Rogue Presidenting

"I CAN COMMAND A BODY OF MEN IN A ROUGH WAY, BUT I AM NOT FIT TO BE PRESIDENT."

—ANDREW JACKSON, TRYING ON SELF-AWARENESS

Andrew Jackson has a lot in common with Alexander Hamilton. He was orphaned at a young age and grew up in poverty before becoming a soldier, a lawyer, and a national hero (in one version of history, at least). So why doesn't he get his own Broadway show? Because, unlike Hamilton, Jackson was a volatile curmudgeon fueled by rage and white pride. And that doesn't really inspire jaunty dance numbers.

Not only was Jackson a garbage human, he was also a terrible president whose policies weren't worth the $20 bill that Harriet Tubman is shoving him off of. His first priority in office was to jumpstart the forced relocation of Native Americans with the aptly named Indian Removal Act of 1830. The Supreme Court ruled against his pet project, but he went for it anyway, ordering the Cherokee of Georgia out of their homes at gunpoint and marching them to reservations via the Trail of Tears. A quarter of them died on the journey. And Jackson, it turns out, was actually committing two crimes against humanity for the price of one by clearing space for more slave plantations. Adding insult to literal human injury, he caused a massive financial crisis before peacing out of the highest office in the land. Nope, no musicals for this guy.

Re: Eternal Damnation

There's nothing a politician hates more than losing the spotlight to someone else, so let's shine one on Lin-Manuel Miranda's race-inclusive *Hamilton*—with a nonstop marathon.

—Satan

KING LEOPOLD II
★★★★★
for Blood Diamonding

"THERE IS REALLY
NOTHING LEFT FOR US
KINGS EXCEPT MONEY!"

—KING LEOPOLD II, HUMBLY

King Leopold II didn't invent European colonization of Africa—he just did it better than any other smug and self-aggrandizing conquering "hero" with a God complex and a bunch of meaningless medals on their chest. As the monarch of Belgium in the nineteenth century, Leopold was driven by an insatiable desire to make his country a well-funded imperial powerhouse. How do you do that? By subjugating, enslaving, killing, and mutilating as many natives as possible while sucking every valuable thing out of the land you've stolen, of course.

This honey badger in philanthropist's clothing established the ironically named Congo Free State in 1885 by convincing other countries to allow him to own it privately rather than colonizing it under Belgium. The Congo River Basin became his own personal plantation, where he forced its inhabitants to convert to Christianity, mine gold and diamonds, kill elephants for ivory, and clear-cut forests to build rubber farms. Those who resisted were killed. Those who didn't meet their impossible quotas had their limbs amputated. And when this Mensa member realized that people can't do his evil bidding without hands, he'd cut up their wives and kids instead. All told, about 15 million people died under his command and a nice, round 100 percent of the profits went directly to ol' Leopold himself.

Re: Eternal Damnation

The great Christian "missionary" will work in Hell's actively burning coal mines toward a quota he'll never meet, getting his limbs chopped off daily for failing. Like the cold-blooded reptile he is, he'll grow them back to be lopped off again the next day.

—Satan

CECIL RHODES

for Colonialism

Today, all the cool teens stream themselves playing video games and performing silly dances. But apparently, back in the 1870s, the trend for rich British teens was taking your inheritance and heading to South Africa to get in on the burgeoning diamond-mining business. (Kids are a lot smarter than they get credit for!) That's what seventeen-year-old Cecil Rhodes did. And he didn't just want a piece of that shiny diamond pie—he set his sights on the whole bakery.

With Slytherin-like strategy, Rhodes spent years collecting mines and creating alliances with the goal of taking over the ruthless De Beers diamond cartel. And he succeeded, becoming the company's chairman in 1888. But the money went to Rhodes's head, and this diehard imperialist decided that he was God's gift to the African people. Their white savior helped deliver them from themselves by (*checks notes*) putting them to work in the mines and stealing their land under the banner of his British South Africa Company. The beacon of humility even named two new colonies after himself: Northern and Southern Rhodesia (modern-day Zambia and Zimbabwe, respectively). But it was all for the native Africans—the ones who would spend the next century trying to scrub Rhodes's name and legacy of colonialism and apartheid from their country.

Re: Eternal Damnation

```
Cecil spent his life feeling like he wasn't doing
enough, so he'll spend eternity in paperwork purgatory,
trying to sort indecipherable forms and navigate
nonsensical red tape to no avail.
```

–Satan

TALAAT PASHA

★★★★★
for **Killer Organizational Skills**

"THE DESTINATION OF THE DEPORTATION IS ANNIHILATION."

—TALAAT PASHA, SAYING THE QUIET PART OUT LOUD

If Talaat Pasha had a LinkedIn profile, it would have his 1917 promotion from chairman to grand vizier (prime minister) of the Ottoman Empire front and center. But this guy's dating profile would pop more red flags than a crypto bro's. Pasha's favorite achievement—and the one he would totally brag about over drinks—was orchestrating the Armenian genocide while serving as Minister of Interior Affairs. (This is why you check all the socials before the appetizers arrive.)

Armenians had lived as a persecuted minority in the Ottoman Empire for decades, surviving two massacres in the 1890s and early 1900s. But after suffering huge losses in the Balkan Wars of the 1910s, Pasha's political party feared Armenians would want independence. Pasha, like most politicians, could spot a good cover for his nefarious deeds. While the world was busy fighting in World War I in 1914 and 1915, the Ottomans got busy rounding up Armenians. On Pasha's deranged orders, more than a million were marched to their deaths in the Syrian desert, starved, dehydrated, tortured, raped, and murdered. Pasha met his karmic end just six years later at the hands of an Armenian student, whose jury patted him on the back as they acquitted him, probably.

Re: Eternal Damnation

What politician doesn't like a play on words? For massacring the residents of modern-day Turkey, Talaat gets to be wrangled, stripped, stuffed, and roasted for Hell's big Thanksgiving dinner every year—when he's not walking aimlessly in our deserts, that is.

—Satan

IMPATIENT PASSENGER

★★☆☆☆
for Blatant Disrespect

Some people just can't play by the rules of logic and sensible row-by-row disembarkation. And by refusing to do so, they engender chaos, gridlock, stress, and frustration all around them. One of the worst offenders? The impatient and self-important travelers who jump lines, crowd other passengers, and generally act like jerks. Guaranteed, these are the same people who ignore a merge lane on the highway, zoom right up to the front, and then try to force their way in.

Does their brutish behavior get them anything but side-eye? Does it speed up the seemingly endless gauntlet of security checks? Of course not. Those TSA agents earned their (hidden) tails in Hell, too. And their fellow passengers are in no mood for it. They're never going to let you cut in line, rusher who is in boarding group C but hovers by the check-in station with group A. You're not going to get off the plane any sooner, guy who stands up in the aisle immediately upon landing, loudly sighing in an attempt to passive-aggressively pressure everybody else to get out of your way. Your Basic Economy ticket does not make you more important than anyone else, Rockefeller. You're just going to have to wait your turn.

Re: Eternal Damnation

These overbearing oafs get the middle seat on an endless red-eye flight, stuck between a guy clipping his toenails and a screaming baby.

—Satan

J. EDGAR HOOVER

★★★☆☆
for Fearmongering

"THE BUREAU OF INVESTIGATION IS NOT CONCERNED WITH POLITICAL MATTERS."

—J. EDGAR HOOVER, JUST FLAT-OUT LYING

How did a paranoid, Red Scare–era spook keep his job as head of the FBI through ten presidents and radically changing and progressing times? A corrupt coward's best weapons: fearmongering and blackmail. J. Edgar Hoover illegally spied and kept files on anyone he didn't like, alleging communist ties, getting people fired, breaking up marriages, and generally acting like a cartoon villain. Under his direction, the FBI even wiretapped Dr. Martin Luther King Jr.'s hotel rooms and sent his wife tapes of his infidelities.

Hoover also worked closely with one of the only people more paranoid than himself—longtime friend Richard Nixon—to take down their enemies and get away with it. The only good thing about the guy was his taste in women's clothing, but keeping his drag persona a secret while weaponizing his puritanical views on human sexuality makes him a hypocrite of the highest caliber. Was he fired when all of his shady behavior came to light? Of course not. Was he fired because he was getting up there in years, napping in his office, and being unapologetically offensive? Still no. Why? Because Nixon was terrified of the man's unhinged willingness to burn it all down. So Hoover died director of the FBI.

Re: Eternal Damnation

The man who dealt in secrets gets to spend his eternity hopelessly out of the loop in a never-ending game of telephone where he gets tantalizingly close to the truth but is constantly interrupted.

—Satan

STROM THURMOND

★★★★☆

for Keeping the Confederate Spirit Alive

> "I AM NOT A RACIST. I AM OPPOSED TO EVERY FORM OF RACISM AND SEGREGATION, EVERY FORM OF DISCRIMINATION."
>
> —STROM THURMOND, DIEHARD RACIST

Familiar with the obnoxious *Looney Tunes* blowhard Foghorn Leghorn? That mashup of Southern clichés is basically the animated embodiment of Senator Strom Thurmond, except Foghorn wasn't an unabashed racist who stuck with his "the South will rise again" shtick until the literal twenty-first century.

Thurmond would feel right at home in modern politics, and for good reason. When the Southern Democrats (today's Republicans) left the 1948 Democratic National Convention in protest against including civil rights in the platform, Thurmond led the charge. He then ran for president as a single-issue, states'-rights candidate, focusing primarily on the "right" to treat Black people like trash. Thurmond lost all the states but managed to get a deeply disturbing 1 million votes.

In 1954, Thurmond used that platform of white supremacy and sneering disdain for Black Americans to win a US Senate seat in South Carolina. He held that position for a horrifying forty-eight years, until 2003, and retired just months before dying at the age of 100 (having tried to will himself to live long enough to avoid his rightful place in Hell). After he died, it was revealed that Thurmond had a Black daughter he loved privately and ignored publicly. Because of course he did.

Re: Eternal Damnation

Eternity wouldn't be long enough for good ol' boy Strom Thurmond to see the error of his ways, so he'll get to spend it straining against cognitive dissonance in a library filled exclusively with great works of literature, music, and film by Black artists.

—Satan

RICHARD NIXON

for Sloppy Secrets

"I AM NOT A CROOK."

—RICHARD NIXON, DEFINITE CROOK

Probably one of the most paranoid and self-loathing squares ever to become President of the United States, Richard Nixon spent his career taking Ls on the national stage before finding his footing as a war criminal. He won the presidency on a "law and order" platform at the height of the Vietnam War. Rather than acknowledge the writing on the wall, a grumbling Nixon escalated the war with the wildly grasping excuse of halting the spread of communism.

But Nixon's not rotting in Hell for being unpopular or shortsighted. No, he earned his spot properly: by bombing unsuspecting innocents, supporting violent dictators, and screwing over people of color. Nixon conspired with his advisers to secretly unleash bombs on Laos and Cambodia, killing millions of civilians in the midst of an already illegal and controversial war. He also provided weapons to the shah of Iran and fascist Augusto Pinochet, who staged bloody revolutions in Iran and Chile, respectively. *And* he started the "war on drugs," which adviser John Ehrlichman admitted was essentially a ruse to put as many Black men and hippies in prison as possible. Through it all, Nixon secretly recorded his racist, meandering, panicked thoughts, which would come back to haunt him during the Watergate scandal that ended his presidency in disgrace.

Re: Eternal Damnation

Sartre once said, "Hell is other people." It certainly will be for Tricky Dick, who gets to room with a guy named Doobie—the most stereotypical hippie who ever lived, who never stops talking about Jefferson Airplane and the Vietnam War.

—Satan

Augusto Pinochet

for Couping

Talk about an insubordinate employee. In 1973, president of Chile, Salvador Allende, promoted prominent military figure Augusto Pinochet to the rank of commander in chief of the country's entire armed forces. And what did he do to show his gratitude for having Chile's entire military might at his disposal? He overthrew the government in a forceful coup just a month after his appointment. And he did it with the support of the US government, who opposed Allende's political leanings and fortified the Chilean military with hush-hush funds and weaponry.

But like most leaders who came to power via violent mutiny, Pinochet wasn't a particularly wholesome guy. And he certainly didn't subscribe to his predecessor's socialist ideologies—namely, thinking everyone was equal. He spent his twenty-five years in power resisting numerous attempts to overthrow him, in part by imprisoning, torturing, or just straight-up murdering anyone he didn't agree with. All told, that amounted to about 40,000 people. The whole thing was pretty embarrassing for the US government, who tried to clean up their mess by urging Pinochet to lighten up on the human-rights abuses. Combined with pressure from many, many other sources, Pinochet finally agreed to allow his people a chance to vote him out. Despite an on-brand attempt to rig the election and intimidate voters, he lost.

Re: Eternal Damnation

This extra-spicy Chilean will be force-fed the spiciest, most colon-blowing chili peppers in the world, including a few that haven't been discovered yet. It'll be like a never-ending episode of *Hot Ones*, but without the pleasant chitchat or heat-quenching milk.

—Satan

IDI AMIN

★★★★★
for Epic Megalomania

"I AM THE HERO OF AFRICA."
—IDI AMIN, UNIVERSALLY HATED IN AFRICA

Never underestimate a delusional narcissist! Ugandan president Milton Obote briefly leaves the country to attend a summit in 1971, and his own head of the military takes it upon himself to overthrow the government in a bloody coup like a Marvel villain. Idi Amin not only had as many of Obote's supporters, government officials, and officers offed as his henchmen could get their hands on, he also ordered his hit squads to kill anyone he considered too liberal, thoughtful, critical, old, or just plain gross. That included—but was not limited to—attorneys, journalists, college students, gay people, and the elderly.

Amin's regime killed so many people that they actually ran out of graveyard space and started feeding the dead to the crocodiles in the Nile River. But even the crocs had their limits, so corpses floated downstream and blocked intake ducts at the country's hydroelectric plants, causing widespread power outages. Adding insult to insanity, Amin collapsed Uganda's economy by expelling the country's entire Asian population (who made up the majority of the workforce). So he didn't really earn his self-proclaimed title of "His Excellency President for Life, Field Marshal Al Hadji Doctor Idi Amin, VC, DSO, MC, CBE, Lord of all the Beasts of the Earth and Fishes of the Sea, and Conqueror of the British Empire in Africa in General and Uganda in Particular" before being overthrown and exiled.

Re: Eternal Damnation

Hell is full of medals commemorating fake achievements and titles, and Idi can have them all—applied directly to his body, though, and not some uniform.

–Satan

Efraín Ríos Montt

for a Good Run

> "I KNOW THAT PRESIDENT RÍOS MONTT IS A MAN OF GREAT PERSONAL INTEGRITY AND COMMITMENT."
>
> —PRESIDENT RONALD REAGAN, HISTORICALLY GOOD JUDGE OF CHARACTER

Efraín Ríos Montt wasn't a normal dictator. He was a *cool* dictator. After all, you really have to go the extra mile to differentiate yourself when you're only in power for seventeen months during an epically long civil war. Guatemala was twenty-two years into that *thirty-six-year* dustup when Montt, unhappy with life under martial law à la General Romeo Lucas Garcia, staged his coup to become acting president. But he didn't do anything to stop the fighting; instead, he egged it on to make himself more powerful.

During his brief time at the helm, Montt focused publicly on rebuilding Guatemala—but he just couldn't seem to find the time for it between killing insurgents, enemies, and anyone who disagreed with him or got in his way. The former military officer's true priority was hobbling the communist guerrillas seeking to overthrow his own corrupt military junta. Under his "leadership," the country experienced a state-sponsored massacre every month from March to December 1982. He had 10,000 people killed in the first three months alone. (OK, maybe he *was* a normal dictator.) But it wasn't long before all that instability caught up with him and he was overthrown by another military subgroup. Still, he lived to the ripe old age of 91—while on trial for crimes against humanity.

Re: Eternal Damnation

Montt thinks *guerillas* are bad? Wait until he meets his new roommate: a 600-pound *gorilla*. Oh, and he'll be trading in his military uniform for a gorilla suit. That should be fun.

–Satan

THE PEOPLE YOU MEET IN HELL

CHILDREN'S RECORDER ADVOCATE

★★★★☆

for Crimes Against Music

Music is, of course, an important and wonderful thing. Without guitars, for example, degenerates would roam the lands and cause chaos, and we wouldn't have been blessed by the song stylings of Chumbawamba. Music education in schools is even more important—it's crucial to childhood development. And, you know, general happiness. But who in their clearly wrong and befuddled mind thought, "What if we made something like a flute but with none of the nuance so it just sounds like a beat-up teapot no matter what you play"? And what masochist decided to give this impossible-to-play instrument to a bunch of kids who have no idea what they're doing and make them spend months of their formative grade-school years trying to eke out a tune? The results are painful and irritating to the point of giving kids a lifelong aversion to playing music and making listeners want to commit murder—or at least assault and battery of a musical instrument. The instrument's inventor may not have had any nefarious intent, but the person who thought it was a good idea to sell cheap recorders to schools certainly deserves a spot in Hell.

Re: Eternal Damnation

Anyone who advocates giving earsplitting instruments to children gets a special set of permanent Bluetooth headphones that allows them to hear those instruments being played, whenever and wherever children are playing them.

—Satan

Saddam Hussein

★★★★★
for Terrorizing the Middle East

S ome dudes are hell-bent on grabbing power and willing to start bloody wars to get it. Saddam Hussein pretty much did the opposite. Conquering new lands for Iraq and creating a campaign of forced worship were mere by-products of the vicious operations he loved. Like an imperialist with a flag, this guy was a big fan of rolling up on other countries and saying, "This is mine now." And anyone who got in the way—or, really, existed in his general vicinity—became collateral damage.

"I CALL ON YOU NOT TO HATE, BECAUSE HATE DOES NOT LEAVE SPACE FOR A PERSON TO BE FAIR AND IT MAKES YOU BLIND AND CLOSES ALL DOORS OF THINKING."

—SADDAM HUSSEIN, HISTORICALLY OPEN-MINDED GUY

In 1959, Saddam was part of the hardline Baath Party who tried to murder the country's dictator. They faceplanted hard, but they tried, tried again, and succeeded in the late 1960s with a jail-hardened Saddam at the helm. He became president of Iraq in 1979, promptly installing posters of himself around town and starting a war with Iran. When he got bored with that, he ordered the deaths of his enemies and—achieving every father's dream—his deadbeat-actor son-in-law. But invading Kuwait in 1990 put him in America's well-equipped crosshairs. This guy became as loathsome to the States as Hitler, but with a way bigger pornstache. So George W. Bush finished what his daddy started, ordering Saddam's capture and then sleeping through his 2006 execution. (On brand for Dubs.)

Re: Eternal Damnation

Saddam loved a selfie. His fellow Iraqis, not so much. Because his mural here in Hell gets vandalized on the regular, he can have a front-row seat—trapped inside the art.

—Satan

SLOBODAN MILOŠEVIĆ

★★★★☆
for Ethnic Cleansing

"THERE IS NO DOUBT WHATSOEVER THAT THE SERBIAN PEOPLE ARE THE FREEST IN THE WORLD."

—SLOBODAN MILOŠEVIĆ, NOTORIOUS FREE-SPEECH ENTHUSIAST

Back in the '90s, Yugoslavia was a country consisting of formerly independent states brought together as one nation under a fragile unity that was constantly challenged by ethnic and religious divisions. (Sound familiar?) After the fall of corrupt communist leader Josip Tito, who was holding the country together with duct tape and suppression, the country endeavored to break up as peacefully as possible. While the primarily Muslim region of Bosnia was looking for independence, its ethnically Serbian population was looking to move over to Serbia.

Now, that's all very tricky stuff, but a diplomatic solution could have been reached. Instead, Serbian president Slobodan Milošević woke up and chose violence. He invited Radovan Karadžić, leader of the Bosnian Serb contingent, to march soldiers into the Bosnian capital of Sarajevo and then bombed it to bits over the course of a four-year siege, laying waste to the beautiful city's ancient buildings and new(ish) infrastructure for the 1984 Winter Olympics alike. Thousands of Muslims were killed in that first round of what governments and the media like to call "ethnic cleansing," which is really just a euphemism for "civil war–related holocaust." Like a Boomer breaking up a fight between siblings, NATO stepped in and gave both factions something to cry about. Their air strikes eventually put an end to the conflict (the murdery part of it, at least). Milošević escaped conviction for war crimes by dying of a heart attack during his trial.

Re: Eternal Damnation

The expert on ethnic cleansing gets to be Hell's new janitor, and boy are our toilets filthy!

—Satan

MUAMMAR GADDAFI

★★★★☆

for State-Sponsored Terrorism

"I WILL NEVER LEAVE LIBYA, I WILL DIE AS A MARTYR AT THE END."

—MUAMMAR GADDAFI, ONE FOR TWO

Gathafi. Kadafi. Kadafi. Gadafy. Qadaffi. Any way you spell (or misspell) it, Muammar Gaddafi spelled trouble for the people of Libya and the world community. When he took power in the early 1970s, Gaddafi drew a hard line regarding who could and could not do business in Libya. And he kicked pretty much anyone who wasn't Libyan over that line to assert the country's sovereignty, including foreign oil conglomerates. That may seem like a patriotic move, but the North African nation was literally bursting with valuable oil. Gaddafi claimed it—and its profits—for Libya and then used them to fuel his lavish lifestyle while his countrymen lived in squalor and suppression.

Few people could unite Cold War adversaries mid-war, but everyone agreed that Gaddafi was bad news. With nowhere else to turn (or maybe because he felt like it), he allied himself with large terrorist organizations, supporting and funding hijackings and bombings like that of the 1988 Pan Am flight that killed 270 people. His violent regime had gotten good at quashing dissidents, but the Arab Spring protests were the straw that broke the authoritarian camel's back. Libyan rebel forces, maddened by Gaddafi's rule, found him hiding in a storm drain after his convoy was captured trying to flee his beloved country, killed him, and dragged his body through the streets to cheers.

Re: Eternal Damnation

Gaddafi's on duck-scrubbing duty, carefully cleansing each innocent creature impacted by the oil industry with his own toothbrush. Whether or not he wants clean teeth, too, is up to him.

—Satan

HISTORICALLY EVIL

CAIN

★★★★★
for Fratricide

"THEREFORE WHOSOEVER SLAYETH CAIN, VENGEANCE SHALL BE TAKEN ON HIM SEVENFOLD."

—GOD, INVENTIVE PUNISHER

The premeditated taking of another's life (aka murder) is an idea so averse to humanity—so toxic, wrong, and foul—that somebody actually had to invent it. Even the most vicious animals don't kill each other for sport or jealousy. And obviously they don't have money or the concept of Mondays to make them feel murderous. But one guy carved out a gruesome difference between man and animal.

Cain, a pivotal character early in the Bible, is credited with being history's first murderer, which is quite a legacy. It must have been something to have been the first guy to say, "Hey, what if I just *don't* wait for nature to take its course, or let God—with whom I have a close working relationship—take care of it? What if I just kill my brother for stealing my thunder?" But that's exactly what Cain did, inventing murder and, by extension, the first murder victim all because his brother, Abel, one-upped his offering to God. Cain offered a sheaf of wheat while Abel offered Him some delicious lamb shanks, and God "looked with favor on Abel." (Dads always have a favorite.) What sibling's blood wouldn't boil? Murder might have been a bit of an overreaction to jealousy, but Cain ran so Jan Brady could walk.

Re: Eternal Damnation

Cain is the perfect guy to head up Hell's Big Brother program, keeping tabs on all of history's worst brothers (Cain, John Wilkes Booth, Attila the Hun, etc.).

–Satan

THE PEOPLE YOU MEET IN HELL

GILLES DE RAIS

★★★★★
for Perversion

Joan of Arc is a household name in the Western world, even outside her native France. Quick refresher: As a teenager, Joan heard the voice of God telling her to lead France in a war to end all wars against rival England. She fought bravely, France won, and she was burned at the stake by the English for—no joke—not adhering to the standards of femininity set by Catholic priests in the 1400s. (And claiming to have regular convos with God didn't help her case with a bunch of guys who'd obviously been ghosted by the Big Guy.) What you might not know is that, during the war, Joan was assisted by an older, more experienced military mind: Gilles de Rais.

In 1440, de Rais was captured and executed just like Joan of Arc, but by the French. Why? Well, it had become clear just why he was so interested in traveling with a 14-year-old girl. He was convicted of raping, torturing, and often murdering as many as 800 children he had encountered as the war raged around France. Before becoming human tinder, de Rais had grown increasingly concerned with saving his own immortal skin (to no avail, obviously). He financed construction of the Chapel of the Holy Innocents—a church he personally staffed with a boys' choir—as an act of penance. (Or maybe convenience?)

Re: Eternal Damnation

I have the perfect place for Gilles—the Smoldering Pines retirement home, where he'll be surrounded by only the most grotesque old folks. Enjoy the prune juice, buddy!

—Satan

TOMÁS DE TORQUEMADA

for Fervor

> "THE INQUISITION
> IS A NECESSARY EVIL."
>
> —TOMÁS DE TORQUEMADA, CLEARLY FUZZY
> ON THE DETAILS OF HIS FAITH

Despite inspiring one of the funniest *Monty Python* sketches in history, the Spanish Inquisition was a real nasty operation. It was created by papal decree in Spain in 1478, supposedly to spread and maintain Catholicism, but it didn't exactly follow the Catholic principle of doing good works. Instead, it was used to root out heretics (read: Jews) like a mob boss might root out rats—without mercy. The Catholic monarchs at the time, King Ferdinand II and Queen Isabella, knew just the guy for the job.

Tomás de Torquemada, a Catholic friar, was given the frightening-sounding office of Grand Inquisitor of the Tribunal of the Holy Office, and apparently he was exempt from consequences for all the sins he committed while working. Convinced that non-Christians were an active threat to the daily life and political structure of Spain, Torquemada helped the monarchs whip up sort of an early anti-immigration sentiment and, in 1492, the crown made being not Christian illegal. And there was no "innocent until proven guilty" in those days. Suspected heretics were brutally and inventively tortured via the rack, the strappado, and that timeless classic: waterboarding. More than 150,000 Jews alone were forced to flee the country or face burning at the stake.

Re: Eternal Damnation

Torquemada can spend eternity unsuccessfully attempting to dodge Monty Python's killer rabbits, holy hand grenades, and absurdly persistent knights.

—Satan

Loose–Change Payers

for Manipulating Time

The fact that coins still exist when we have credit cards, mobile payments, and even crypto (make-believe as it may be) is already baffling. That there are people out there who think it's perfectly acceptable to pay their entire bill with those coins? Unbelievable. First, they insist on paying in germy cash just so they can fill that cheddar-dusted Costco jug with coins. Then, instead of taking the coins to a bank like a normal person, they head to the store with full pockets and a mission to annoy as many people as possible.

Even before they reach for the coins, you hear the jingling orchestra of copper and silver and know what's coming. With each scrape of metal, the line behind you stretches and everyone in it contemplates their life choices. How did you end up here, in a realm where time slows down and patience becomes a distant memory? At a time in history when coin-counting machines exist and stores insist on opening a single register for dozens of customers, paying with loose change is an act of violence. It's like the coin holder is fueled by the agonized sighs of all those stuck behind them and the cashier's sanity slipping away, one nickel at a time. But they will pay for their crimes—and not in nickels.

Re: Eternal Damnation

Those who pay for anything more than cheap black coffee in loose change are doomed to work the checkout counters of Hell. You think you were a difficult customer? Just wait.

–Satan

CHRISTOPHER COLUMBUS

"WITH 50 MEN THEY CAN ALL BE SUBJUGATED AND MADE TO DO WHAT IS REQUIRED OF THEM."

—CHRISTOPHER COLUMBUS,
MILD-MANNERED TOURIST

★ ☆ ☆ ☆ ☆
for Navigational Skills

The fact that Christopher Columbus got a federal holiday in his honor is a testament to the victors writing the history books. They managed to make people think he discovered a country he didn't while ignoring all the serial-killeresque stuff that he actually did. (If cell phones were around to record this guy when he "discovered America," he would have been thrown into solitary wearing a straitjacket and a muzzle.)

When Columbus landed *in the Bahamas* in 1492 with fame and fortune in his sights, he was met with warmth and curiosity from the indigenous Taíno people. But, noticing that these folks didn't have iron weapons, the psychopath decided to enslave them. On one of his four voyages (not one of which made it to North America), Columbus kidnapped 1,000 people, enslaving about half locally and sending the rest back to Spain; 200 of them died on the trip. He forced every Taíno over the age of fourteen on Hispaniola (now Haiti and the Dominican Republic) to deliver an impossible amount of gold; 50,000 chose mass suicide over submitting to the Spaniards. Within sixty years of Columbus's arrival, the native population had been almost entirely wiped out by European colonialism and disease. Totally worth closing the banks on a Monday 600 years later, right?

Re: Eternal Damnation

Columbus gets the *Groundhog Day* treatment with a broken GPS that constantly says "recalculating" while it drives him to his doom in a thousand different ways: off a cliff, into a volcano, into a tribe of cannibals, into a tank full of piranhas, and so on and so on.

—Satan

DOG HATER

★★★☆☆
for Being Dead Inside

Few creatures on earth are as joyful, loving, and pure as dogs. They're smart, loyal, goofy, furry, and adorable—and that's just to start. They're also hard workers, lifesaving heroes, and nonjudgmental cheerleaders. (A dog will be more supportive of your Etsy aspirations than any blood relative.) And all they ask in return for their undying love and companionship is some kibble and the occasional scratch behind the ears. Dogs are so great that even cat people love them (and they have some notoriously high standards when it comes to companionship).

So how is it possible that some people say, "I'm just not a dog person"? You don't like love? You can't appreciate warm snuggles? You don't want someone to save you if you've fallen down a well? If it's the daily walks that turn you off, you could probably use someone to help you get your butt off the couch. And if you're going to let a little hot poop get between you and a literal angel on Earth, you need to do some inner work on yourself. Go to the shelter and get a dog to help you with it.

Re: Eternal Damnation

If you can't be kind to dogs in life, you'll spend eternity making it up to them by knitting them adorable little sweaters. (And if you're someone who takes their frustrations and insecurities out on those warm and wonderful creatures? Even the depths of Hell are too good for you. You'll be reassigned to Florida.)

—Satan

Francisco Pizarro

for Brutally Successful Conquesting

> "I CAME TO SERVE GOD AND
> THE KING, AND TO GET RICH AS
> ALL MEN WANT TO DO."
>
> —FRANCISCO PIZARRO, MAN OF HONOR

Hey, early sixteenth-century kids, have you heard about the latest craze that's sweeping Europe? It's called "exploring the New World"! But don't let that name all full of curiosity and wonder confuse you. It actually refers to a military-like conquest funded by royals with egos bigger than their castles. With their flag hoisted, you'll set sail to the Americas and steal the land and all of its valuable treasures from societies that have been there for hundreds of years. Fun!

For Francisco Pizarro, that meant using funds from King Charles V of Spain to conquer what is now Peru (originally Tawantinsuyu) in the name of that Iberian powerhouse. Pizarro landed in 1532 and invited the local ruler, King Atahualpa of the Incas, to a celebratory feast in his honor. We all know where this is going. Atahualpa learned the hard way never to trust a conquistador in a ridiculous hat— it was an ambush. Pizarro kidnapped the king and had his men slaughter 5,000 unarmed Incas in about an hour. Atahualpa negotiated his release, agreeing to give Pizarro enough gold to fill a room. Pizarro agreed and then reneged on his promise as soon as he had received his spoils, killing most of the Incas that remained, ending the largest ancient civilization in pre-Columbian America, and setting up South America to be colonized by Spain for the next 300+ years. Yay, exploration!

Re: Eternal Damnation

To give Frank a sense of what it feels like to be attacked while unarmed, demons posing as Incans will rip off his arms and then beat him with them.

–Satan

Elizabeth Báthory

for Cosmetic Vampirism

Unless you were a peasant faced with a life of constant toil, subsistence farming, and burying children who died of starvation, there wasn't much to do in Hungary at the turn of the seventeenth century. The wealthy ruling class, to which Countess Elizabeth Báthory belonged, didn't need to work. So how did the countess kill time? By killing others. And she got away with it because authorities shrugged off losing a few hundred servants and peasants.

Like something out of a particularly unclever horror movie, "The Blood Countess" earned her nickname by living and killing inside of a castle she'd outfitted with a torture chamber and filled with girls kidnapped from surrounding towns. While they were still alive, Báthory would do things like bite off and consume pieces of their flesh and shove needles under their nails. When she was finished playing with her food, she'd drain her captives of their blood until they were dead. Why? Aside from your run-of-the-mill psychopathic tendencies, Báthory believed drinking the blood of young women gave her a youthful glow. (Who knows—maybe she wouldn't have been so murderous had La Mer been invented just a few centuries earlier.) It wasn't until Báthory started killing nobles that anyone cared. In 1611, she was convicted of only eighty murders and given house arrest . . . in her castle.

Re: Eternal Damnation

You're so vain, Liz, which is why you get to spend eternity in a room filled with Dorian Gray-like mirrors, reflecting you old, ugly, and on your worst hair day.

—Satan

CATHERINE DE' MEDICI

for Meddling

"I WOULD RATHER MY SON REIGNED FOR ONE YEAR IN PEACE THAN FOR FORTY YEARS IN WAR."

—CATHERINE DE' MEDICI, REDEFINING "PEACE"

No matter how much you complain about your mom's meddling ways, she has nothing on Catherine de' Medici. Born to a wealthy family who ruled Florence (and most of its banks), de' Medici consolidated her family's power by marrying the future Henry II of France in 1533. She bore three French kings (plus seven spares). A staunch Catholic who didn't much care for the rising population of Huguenots (Protestants who believed exactly the same religious principles as Catholics, minus fealty to a pope), she ordered the death of a French Protestant leader. When the assassination flopped, de' Medici slipped her son Charles IX false intel about a Protestant uprising.

Impressionable mama's boy that he was, Charles planned and orchestrated the murder of all the prominent French Protestant leaders (who were in town for his own sister's wedding, by the way). The rest of Catholic France took that royal act as a signal to start hauling Huguenots out of their homes and killing them in what became known as the St. Bartholomew's Day Massacre. Within a year, 70,000 Protestant men, women, and children throughout France were dead and civil war was raging in France—all because of one meddlesome mom.

Re: Eternal Damnation

Everyone gets roasted in Hell, but Cathy gets her own personal Comedy Central–style roast—complete with demons telling pointed and hilarious jokes at her expense. They really hurt her feelings.

—Satan

GILLES GARNIER

★★★★☆
for Pioneering Lycanthropy

In 1572, kids from the French village of Dole started to go missing. But authorities soon realized that this wasn't an ordinary kidnapping case. The children were later found in the woods on the outskirts of the town—or at least parts of them were. Because this was the sixteenth century, town elders took their mangled and strewn limbs to mean that Dole had a werewolf in its midst. They authorized the citizenry to hunt and kill the beast, Gaston style—and they found him.

Local hermit Gilles Garnier was standing over the body of a freshly killed child when the mob discovered him. Garnier confessed to feasting on four children but was quick to point out that a demon had offered him an ointment that would turn him into a hunting machine so he could feed himself and his wife. *So it totally wasn't even his fault, you guys.* Still, Garnier was convicted of murder as well as criminal werewolfism (which was apparently a thing in premodern France) and burned alive. The freaked-out townspeople even scattered his ashes to the winds for good measure. After all, you can never be too careful when it comes to contagious mythical illnesses spread by demons.

Re: Eternal Damnation

If Gilles is going to pretend to be a murderous werewolf, he can do it in Hell's live production of Michael Jackson's classic music video for "Thriller." Let's see those jazz claws!

—Satan

CARLO GESUALDO

for **Unprincely Behavior**

In the late sixteenth century, Italian prince Carlo Gesualdo balanced his schedule of being idly rich with a career as an avant-garde composer. He wrote ominous, moody, and unsettling works because, as the saying goes, you write what you know. Gesualdo had a lot of darkness (read: insanity) inside, and he exorcised it with not just music but also witchcraft and murder.

In October 1590, Gesualdo caught his wife, Maria d'Avalos, in the middle of a passionate moment with Fabrizio Carafa, the Duke of Andria. Having known about the affair and set up the encounter himself, he immediately killed them both in thorough and spectacular fashion. He riddled the handsome duke with gunshot and stab wounds, while he beat the little missus and slashed her throat, possibly with the help of some of his servants. Witnesses saw Gesualdo enter the lovers' nest, shouting, and then reemerge covered in blood, only to go back in and make sure he finished the job. Some accounts say that he even displayed the mutilated bodies outside the palace afterward. But apparently, being rich and cuckolded entitled you to certain acts of revenge in those days. So instead of going to jail, Gesualdo remarried, acquired a mistress, did some witchy rituals to cure his crazy, and got back to writing weird music that nobody wanted to hear. But he spent his remaining years in isolation, eliciting the same hushed tones and wary looks from locals as the guy who talks to imaginary pigeons on the subway does.

Re: Eternal Damnation

The so-called Prince of Darkness (how *dare* they!) can spend eternity playing faithful and happy househusband to Marie Antoinette. Be careful with those wigs, Carlo!

–Satan

Revenge Porn Uploader

★★☆☆☆
for Being Gross

It should come as no surprise that the residents of Hell, The Place Where Sinning Is In™, are a sex-positive bunch. They tacitly approve of porn as long as it's between consenting adults—that's why they have annual passes to all the conventions. As an industry, it's right up there with gambling and American beer. People peddling lust, temptation, greed, and gluttony? Count them in. But they're not here for Todd's revenge porn, which takes something lovely, like drunken boning, and makes it ugly.

People in all situationships should feel free to send each other sexy snaps and tasteful nudes without fear of them living on the Internet forever for all the world and their future bosses to see. And when one person is so butt-hurt by a breakup or so callous about a hookup that they choose to humiliate the photographee online, they ruin the good name of porn for everyone. Just be glad that it happened, delete those pics, and cherish those very vivid memories. It's called being a mature adult, Todd.

Re: Eternal Damnation

Todd and his callous friends can learn what it's like to be on the receiving end of a breach of privacy with video billboards of their worst and most humiliating moments scattered all over Hell.

—Satan

CHRISTMAN GENIPPERTEINGA

★★★★★
for Legendary Skills

All of those dark, centuries-old folktales from the Black Forest of Germany had one thing in common: seeds of truth. True monsters lurked in those woods, too, like Christman Genipperteinga. This rogue Robin Hood of the late 1500s executed a thirteen-year-long campaign of terror on the general public, remorselessly robbing and killing unsuspecting passersby on the regular. Like a murderous Barney Stinson, Genipperteinga is said to have kept a log of conquests with an end-goal in mind: 1,000 kills. And he nearly made it. When he was executed via limb-ripping wheel in 1581, he was at 964. (Barney's goal of 200 looks downright reasonable in comparison, especially when you account for population density.)

Legend has it that six of those victims were Genipperteinga's own children, born to a woman he'd kidnapped and held for seven years. Police caught the cutthroat when that woman escaped his hut and dropped a trail of peas for authorities to follow back to his lair. Or at least, so the story goes. If that all sounds a little too "Hansel and Gretel," it's for good reason. It's the plot of another Grimm tale: "The Robber Bridegroom." In fact, Genipperteinga's biography overlaps with that of several others at a time when roving bands of robbers and killers were a very real threat. So, whether Genipperteinga inspired those stories or his has been embellished over the centuries, he can take the heat.

Re: Eternal Damnation

For being a (possibly) real legend, Christman gets the Snow White treatment—an eternity of playing housemaid to the most gag-inducing demons Hell has.

—Satan

ADRIAAN VALCKENIER

for Business Savvy

> "WE MUST MAINTAIN GOOD RELATIONS WITH THE LOCAL POPULATIONS AND RESPECT THEIR CUSTOMS AND TRADITIONS."
>
> —ADRIAAN VALCKENIER, RUTHLESS COLONIZER

You think union-busting is bad today? Jeff Bezos may be a monster for spending company profits on personal space travel instead of a livable wage for his workers, but he still has nothing on Adriaan Valckenier. The general-governor of the Dutch East India Company responded to a totally valid (though, OK, fairly violent) uprising over slave wages with actual genocide.

One of the most powerful companies in history, the Dutch East India Company fueled the imperialist and colonialist whims of European countries for hundreds of years. This wasn't just an eighteenth-century Amazon. The Dutch Republic gave the company license to wage war, make treaties, coin money, and establish colonies, which meant its top dogs were rich, powerful, and above the law. To keep profit margins high, they paid local workers next to nothing. In 1740, the Chinese workers in Batavia, capital of the Dutch East Indies (modern-day Jakarta, Indonesia) revolted in a big way against their de facto slave masters. Adriaan Valckenier responded in kind and then some, ordering his *in-house army* (let's hope modern-day CEOs don't pick up on that one) to attack and kill any and all Chinese people—not just the protesters. Over two weeks, an estimated 10,000 Chinese men, women, children were slaughtered. It's small consolation that the higher-ups also thought Valckenier went too far. He died in prison in the Netherlands.

Re: Eternal Damnation

Valckenier's probably not familiar with the concept of "going Dutch," or splitting a bill. In Hell, that just means slowly being ripped in half.

—Satan

King Yeongjo and Prince Sado

for Toxic Relationships

Believe it or not, the Kims weren't the first dysfunctional bunch of narcissists to grace the leadership rungs of the Korean Peninsula. A good 200 years before war split Korea into two countries, it was one nation ruled by King Yeongjo, with his eldest son, Crown Prince Sado, set to take over. Instead of instilling his son with the confidence and knowledge to rule, King Yeongjo's abusive parenting screwed him up for life.

Whether it was just his daddy issues or an attack of measles that prompted Sado's erratic behavior, historians can't be sure. All they know is that the prince developed some gruesome coping mechanisms. Murder became his stress relief, his happy place, his favorite pastime. By the 1760s, he rarely ventured out of the royal palace; he was busy raping female visitors and killing guests and palace staffers at will. Surviving staff members started hauling out bodies as part of their regular duties—that is, when Sado was done with them. He was known to carry heads around on sticks. Once Sado grew weary of killing strangers and started trying to rape and murder his sister, King Yeongjo decided he'd had enough. Carefully exploiting a loophole in Korean execution laws, he locked his son inside a wooden rice chest to starve to death. Get this man a Father of the Year award!

Re: Eternal Damnation

No two people in history have needed therapy more than these two. And they'll get it—hours and hours of talk therapy led by an expert in attachment parenting.

—Satan

CHARLES TREVELYAN

for Assisting Famine

Pretty much everybody knows that the Irish potato famine killed a lot of people. It also led to the mass exodus of Irish citizens to countries that weren't suffering under agricultural blights and a heartless and remote government. No one could have seen that devastating and naturally occurring fungus coming for Ireland's main food source. But one man could have saved hundreds of thousands of lives if not for his tough-love style of politics.

British civil servant and guy who was definitely not hugged enough as a child Charles Trevelyan *really* hated the people of Ireland. But in the 1840s, the country was under British rule, and he was England's assistant secretary of the Treasury, so the Emerald Isle's plight became his problem. Tens of thousands of people had starved to death, and Trevelyan was tasked with helping in some way. A devout proponent of laissez-faire government, Trevelyan said "no thanks," fearing that aiding the Irish would make them "habitually dependent" on the British government. Not only did he refuse to help, he also shut down anybody else who tried to, even turning away US ships full of food. And a million Irish starved to death. (The man was ahead of his time with that "pull yourself up by your bootstraps" attitude—he'd fit right in with today's politicians.)

Re: Eternal Damnation

Potatoes were God's gift to man. The potato gun was mine. Charley can spend eternity being pelted by potatoes from the guns of thousands of little demons.

—Satan

DELPHINE LaLAURIE

"I WAS A WOMAN OF MY TIME."

—KATHY BATES, SPEAKING FACTS AS LALAURIE
IN *AMERICAN HORROR STORY: COVEN*

for Offending Other Slave Owners

You've got to be pretty despicable if Southern slave owners—people so horrible that the right to own human beings was the hill they literally chose to die on—think you're bad news. Such was the aspersion cast upon ridiculously rich New Orleans resident Delphine LaLaurie. Could part of that side-eye be because she was a wealthy, self-possessed woman in the 1800s? Sure. More likely, it was the fact that she brutally and fatally abused enslaved people for sport instead of just making them work under deplorable and torturous conditions like everyone else did. (How else was a well-to-do person to entertain themselves in those pre-stock-market days?)

In 1833, LaLaurie went full sociopath by chasing an enslaved child onto the roof and whipping her until she plummeted to her death. The police found the child's body thrown into a well and, amazingly for the racist antebellum South, arrested LaLaurie. Although she was compelled to sell off her slaves, she had her relatives buy and return them. But when one such prisoner set fire to the house in an escape attempt, exposing LaLaurie's attic torture chamber to the whole neighborhood, it was game over for the high-society sadist. A mob of other slave owners in town gathered in protest, forcing LaLaurie to flee the country.

Re: Eternal Damnation

Kathy Bates did a masterful job of playing Delphine in *American Horror Story*, but we're not in the business of flattering our residents. So LaLaurie is hereby sentenced to an eternity of watching Bates' worst movie, *Fred Claus*, instead.

—Satan

YOUR DENTIST

★★★☆☆
for Torture

EVERYDAY
MONSTER
BREAK!

What do you call a doctor with a sadistic streak? A dentist! Dentistry has all the trappings of practicing medicine—your own office, a hefty paycheck, a God complex—without any of the late nights or gross intestinal stuff. Plus, you get to pawn all the dirty work off on hygienists and keep all the fun needles and drills for yourself.

Not only do dentists torture their patients physically by boring into their outside bones with power tools, they also play mind games while they do it. They force you to endure long waits, elevator music, and that weird saliva-sucker while making conversation about their sports cars and boats, which you can't engage in because you've got a mouth full of fingers. And then they charge you a fortune because—surprise!— they don't take your insurance. Dentists are doing Satan's work right here on Earth, so it only makes sense that they go home to their master in the end. But he's not exactly an appreciative boss, so think twice about sticking your fingers where they don't belong!

Re: Eternal Damnation

When you've perfected torture, it's only fair that you get to experience it. Dentists endure a never-ending dental procedure with no numbing agents, a water shooter that's freezing cold, an industrial-strength suction thingy, and a very chatty dentist, all with Kenny G blaring overhead.

—Satan

ROXEY ANN CAPLIN

for Toxic Femininity

"CORSETS SHOULD BE DESIGNED TO BE BOTH FASHIONABLE AND HEALTHY."

—ROXEY ANN CAPLIN, THROUGH SHALLOW BREATHS

You would think that the person who created the Victorian corset—an enduring act of mild torture at best and disfigurement at worst that relied on violently tight laces—would totally be a dude. No woman would foist something so uncomfortable on their own sex for the sake of the male gaze, right? Alas, the perpetuator of this misogynistic undergarment is one who knew too well the suffering it would cause: Roxey Ann Caplin. (It only adds insult to very real injury that the inventor's name makes her sound like an empowering, sex-positive influencer.)

In exchange for a streamlined waist and boosted bust, corsets squeeze a woman's bones and organs, slowly morphing the body over time until the organs are displaced like a cat conforming to a small vase. Cats may be shape-shifters, but human organs are not, so corsets can wreak all sorts of havoc on the body, like an inability to breathe or digest food. This crime against the whole of womanhood in the mid-1800s would also feed into toxic beauty standards and messed-up body images for generations. And for what? So Caplin's fellow judgmental, self-loathing Victorians would consider you proper. (Those laces were like a nineteenth-century chastity belt.) Thanks, Roxey!

Re: Eternal Damnation

Oh, Roxey prefers a feminine silhouette? We have just the thing for her—an eternal uniform of Billie Eilish's signature oversized hoodies and baggy sweats.

—Satan

AMELIA DYER

★★★★★
for Resourcefulness

"GOD ALMIGHTY IS MY JUDGE,
AND I DARE NOT GO INTO HIS
PRESENCE WITH A LIE."

—AMELIA DYER, UPSTANDING CHRISTIAN

In the 1890s in England, Amelia Dyer set up what's known as a "baby farming" operation. Just as some people abuse the foster care system by taking in as many children as possible to collect multiple checks from the state to pay for their care, Dyer collected abandoned and orphaned babies for a fee. But the trained nurse had no intention of caring for them. She killed them with liquid opiates or slowly starved them to death, depending on how quickly she wanted to be rid of them. No one knows how many children Dyer killed, but it was likely in the hundreds.

After *several* babies died in her care, Dyer was sentenced to six months of hard labor for the crime of neglect. (Hey, times were tough for babies in Victorian England without modern medicine and mommy bloggers!) But six months wasn't enough for Dyer to learn her lesson. The baby farmer not only resumed operations right after serving her sentence, she started tossing her kills into rivers to get rid of the evidence. When one of those bodies was inevitably traced back to her—because, expert criminal that she was, she padded it with an envelope addressed to her—a death sentence finally put her out of business.

Re: Eternal Damnation

Amelia can spend eternity in Hell's creepiest bed-and-breakfast, in a room surrounded by porcelain dolls, all of them haunted with shrieking spirits and Chucky-like poltergeists.

—Satan

R. J. Reynolds

★ ★ ★ ★ ★
for Multilevel Marketing

Not everything that grows in the ground is good for you—poison ivy, for example. You would never let some giant corporation talk you into lighting poison ivy on fire and inhaling it into your lungs several times a day. You'd also never let them convince you that inhaling literal poison was cool, and that doing so made you look sophisticated. Of course not, because you know it'll kill you. And before it does, it'll make you exhausted, miserable, and smelly. The entire notion is absurd and dangerous, and yet R. J. Reynolds created an entire industry around getting people to do just that with tobacco.

Reynolds became the wealthiest person in the tobacco-farming state of North Carolina by expanding the R. J. Reynolds Tobacco Company into America's chief purveyor and marketer of cigarettes, which still kill half a million people a year in the US despite the stark warning labels. Now, we could give 'ol R. J. the benefit of the doubt. No one could have known in 1875 that smoking caused disease. (Hardly anyone lived long enough in those days to test the theory.) But there's no way the guy thought inhaling flaming plants was *good* for you. And the R. J. Reynolds Tobacco Company continued creating new products and Joe Camel cartoons long after that info came to light and its founder died of pancreatic cancer—a disease caused by, you guessed it, smoking. So, yeah, Hell it is.

Re: Eternal Damnation

Like a kid caught smoking and forced to finish the pack, R. J. Reynolds will spend his afterlife smoking every discarded butt in existence.

—Satan

THE PEOPLE YOU MEET IN HELL

RAYMOND VONDERLEHR

for Spreading Disease

> "THE UNITED STATES GOVERNMENT DID SOMETHING THAT WAS WRONG—DEEPLY, PROFOUNDLY, MORALLY WRONG."
>
> —PRESIDENT BILL CLINTON, GENERALLY APOLOGETIC GUY

"The Tuskegee Experiment" sounds like the name of a futuristic Michael Crichton techno-thriller, or some horrible Nazi thing, but it's actually a deadly four-decade-long study done on American soil under the watchful eye of American government employees. Raymond Vonderlehr wasn't just one of those employees; he was the onsite director of the study from 1932 until 1943 and director of the Centers for Disease Control and Protection from 1947 to 1951. The study's purpose was to observe the effects of syphilis left unchecked. Not to treat it. Not to cure it. Just to watch it like a NASCAR race, secretly hoping for a multicar crash.

Unsurprisingly, Vonderlehr and his staff were pretty tight-lipped about that with the hundreds of African American men they recruited for the study, using the promise of free medical care. Medical care for what, you ask? "Bad blood," a catchall term for a range of ailments. The poor guys didn't even know they had syphilis. And when syph-stopping penicillin came onto the treatment scene in 1943—while Vonderlehr was still onsite director—the study continued, unchanged. By the time it was disbanded in 1972 (and only because the public got wind of it), twenty-eight men had died from syphilis, a hundred more had died from related complications, and the disease had infected at least forty of their spouses and nineteen of their children. So much for disease control and protection!

Re: Eternal Damnation

Turnabout is fair play! Ray gets to suffer the effects of every STD while trapped inside a lab cage like a rat and studied by African American doctors.

—Satan

Your Junior High Gym Teacher

★★★☆☆
for the Schadenfreude

EVERYDAY MONSTER BREAK!

Think carefully about your career choices! Every gym teacher goes to Hell when they die for their many sins against kids who are just trying to make it to French Bread Pizza Fridays. These are people who choose to earn their living by bringing universal trauma to children as a matter of course—or maybe as a perverse source of personal entertainment.

Each day, for decades of their finite and precious existence, they put on their too-tight shorts and force kids to run laps around a soggy field before allowing them to shuffle off, sweaty and winded, to algebra class. But that's not all! They also body-shame them for being too skinny *and* not skinny enough, make them throw balls at each other like sadistic monkeys flinging poop, conduct the Presidential Fitness Exam (invented in Hell in 1982), and then—to add insult to prepubescent injury—make everyone change clothes in front of each other. Phys ed instructors are but an errant black mark on the gymnasium floor of life.

Re: Eternal Damnation

There's no Presidential Fitness Exam like the original! The gym teachers of the world get to spend their eternities climbing the rope in their underwear while being pelted with dodgeballs, waiting for a bell that will never ring to save them. *Suck it up, pipsqueak!*

—Satan

CHARLES PONZI

for Eponymous Scamming

"I LANDED IN THIS COUNTRY WITH $2.50 IN CASH AND $1 MILLION IN HOPES, AND THOSE HOPES NEVER LEFT ME."

—CHARLES PONZI, CHASING THE AMERICAN DREAM

It's pretty cool to accomplish something so massive that it forever bears your name, a lasting legacy that outlives you. It'd be more of a silver lining for Charles Ponzi if his name weren't synonymous with "scams," "schemes," and "multilevel marketing programs selling leggings and candles perpetuated by your most basic high school friends on Facebook." That's gotta hurt.

Ponzi was the original corporate fraudster, a pioneering freelance huckster who, incredibly, wasn't a baron of industry or an internationally lauded tycoon used to pulling the wool over buyers' eyes. The two-time jailbird started his overly confident march to the history books in the early 1920s with—wait for it—mail fraud. The plan was to exploit a favorable exchange rate for postage stamps. He attracted investors by promising huge returns, but all he was doing was borrowing from one lender to pay off another and pocketing what he could in the middle. New investors took care of the old ones until the pyramid scheme collapsed amid the chaos of a *Boston Post* investigation and a run on Ponzi's company. Around 40,000 people lost as much as $20 million, a fiasco that put six pre-FDIC banks out of business and sent Ponzi to prison—again—for fourteen years. He died, divorced and penniless, in Brazil years later.

Re: Eternal Damnation

Ponzi likes pyramids? Great, he can take the base position on Hell's cheer team—on all fours, with demons jumping up and down on him, forever. Big smile, Charlie!

—Satan

THE PEOPLE YOU MEET IN HELL

J. PAUL GETTY

for Bad Blood

> "I HAVE FOURTEEN OTHER GRANDCHILDREN AND IF I PAY ONE PENNY NOW, THEN I WILL HAVE FOURTEEN KIDNAPPED GRANDCHILDREN."
>
> —J. PAUL GETTY, PRAGMATIST

Kidnapping a person is a horrible thing, obviously. But is it worse to refuse to pay a loved one's ransom when you're worth billions of dollars? It's definitely not great. If you're more concerned with pinching pennies than saving a life, you have to ask yourself if the abducted *really is* a loved one. In J. Paul Getty's case, that loved one was his own grandson. Yikes!

Getty, filthy-rich oil tycoon and, at one point, the richest man on Earth, was a tightwad despite billions in mid-century money obtained by bleeding the planet dry and then polluting it. In 1973, his sixteen-year-old grandson, John Paul Getty III, was kidnapped by Mafia types in Italy for a $17 million ransom. The elder Getty initially refused, thinking it was a ruse by the younger Getty to get money out of his stingy grandpa. (Clearly some family drama there.) Then he tried to say it was the kid's own fault for getting kidnapped. Five months of negotiations between the kidnappers and the teen's mom went by before the kidnappers chopped off and mailed Getty's ear to show how serious they were. Finally, Getty talked the criminals down to $3 million. He paid $2 million himself—the most he was legally allowed to write off as a tax deduction—and loaned his son the remaining $1 million with a 4 percent interest rate. How generous!

Re: Eternal Damnation

J. P. barely blinked at his grandson losing an ear, so let's take both of his. Whenever someone tries to warn him against danger, they'll sound like Charlie Brown's teacher.

—Satan

HEINRICH MÜCKTER

★★★★☆
for Rebranding

"WE WISH THAT THE THALIDOMIDE TRAGEDY HAD NEVER HAPPENED."

—GRÜNENTHAL, ATTEMPTING A NON-APOLOGY APOLOGY

After World War II ended, not every Nazi muckety-muck wound up dead in a bunker or in front of an international war crimes tribunal, where they belonged. Heinrich Mückter, who worked at the Auschwitz concentration camp as a doctor and used prisoners as his guinea pigs, managed to escape his just desserts and go on to become the head of research for German drug company Chemie Grünenthal. (Apparently they saw "doctor" on his résumé and didn't do any more digging?) As if he didn't inflict enough harm during his tenure with the SS, Mückter decided to apply his talent for torture to the bumbling live-action game of Operation that was (and still is) women's healthcare.

Mückter developed and got approval for an anti–morning sickness drug for pregnant women called thalidomide. The drug was so potentially profitable that he rushed it to market in 1957 without the kind of trials and testing that keep dangerous drugs off pharmacy shelves. And he received huge bonuses for doing so. (Yep—there's a large Grünenthal contingency straddling embers in Hell.) It took four years for researchers to make the connection between thalidomide and the disfiguring birth defects it caused. By that time, more than 10,000 babies had been born with disfigured or missing limbs. But was Mückter finally held to account? Of course not.

Re: Eternal Damnation

Heinrich is hereby sentenced to an eternity of using the many kinds of birth control that women have endured throughout history. Side effects will vary but are guaranteed.

–Satan

THE PEOPLE YOU MEET IN HELL

WILLIAM B. SHOCKLEY

★★★★★
for Pure Ego

"THE VIEW THAT THE US NEGRO IS INHERENTLY LESS INTELLIGENT THAN THE US WHITE CAME FROM MY CONCERN FOR THE WELFARE OF HUMANITY."

—WILLIAM B. SHOCKLEY,
DEFENDING THE INDEFENSIBLE

William Shockley is one of the most important and influential American inventors of the twentieth century. He headed up the team at Bell Labs that won the 1956 Nobel Prize for Physics for developing the semiconductor and transistor, which led to modern electronics and computing. How did Shockley use his hard-earned intellectual capital and cultural cache? By spewing racist vitriol couched in scientific jargon and then putting his bizarre and destructive ideas into action by supporting a bigoted sperm-bank business. Seems normal.

Shockley started to go off the rails in 1965, writing and giving addresses about how white people were genetically and intellectually superior to Black people. He believed that people of color were reproducing at a higher rate than white people, which obviously spelled doom for the world at large. His proposal: forced sterilization. Did Shockley have any expertise in genetics, biology, or psychology? Nope! He was a white guy in the '60s—he didn't need actual expertise. But as a Nobel Prize winner, he did have the genetic material that eugenics advocate Robert Klark Graham was looking for. Graham owned the Repository for Germinal Choice, colloquially known as the "Nobel Prize Sperm Bank" because he purported to use only swimmers from supersmart Nobel laureates. The only donor ever confirmed? Not shockingly, Shockley, spreading his "superior" seed like the humanitarian he was.

Re: Eternal Damnation

Guess who gets to be reincarnated as a sperm, swimming around a never-ending game of Pac-Man and trying not to get eaten! This guy.

—Satan

Josef Mengele

★★★★★
for Nazi Experimentation

G iving people the encouragement they need to be themselves is great . . . most of the time. But horrible people giving psychopaths permission to let their freak flag fly? Not so much. And boy, did Josef Mengele let that baby fly.

An early adopter of eugenics (the scientifically bogus and wildly racist idea that one kind of people are biologically superior to another), Mengele was all for Adolf Hitler's plans of world domination via extermination of the Jewish people. He got his feet wet determining whether German citizens were purebred enough or destined for forced sterilization, like some kind of demented dog show judge. Later, he served as chief physician at Auschwitz, where he quickly developed a reputation for making the concentration camps even more horrifically ghoulish. His doctoring didn't involve rounds or listening to complaints. The so-called Angel of Death decided whether his "patients" were fit for hard labor, the gas chamber, or—worst of all—his surgical table, where they were subjected to sterilization, vivisection, and infection without the aid of painkillers (so, torture). But Mengele didn't get to finish his work. When the camps fell, the coward bolted and swapped out that freak flag for Argentine, Paraguayan, and Brazilian flags, respectively, before finally drowning in 1979. Better late than never!

Re: Eternal Damnation

Torture, you say? That's our specialty. Josef can lead the charge as Hell's official Creative Punishment Test Subject.

—Satan

THE PEOPLE YOU MEET IN HELL

ANTÓNIO EGAS MONIZ

★ ★ ★ ★ ☆

for Weird Science

Medicine isn't really a science. Oh wait—yes, it is. But before the late twentieth century—yes, the most recent one—treating the various ailments affecting the human body required a mix of trial, error, and an overconfident "fake it till you make it" attitude. Surgeon António Moniz embraced that hit-or-miss combination with open arms, a pioneering spirit, and a distinct lack of remorse for his misses. He believed that the best way to cure mental-health issues was to stab into the brain with a medical-grade ice pick–like thing and just kind of swirl it around and cut things out—a procedure known today as the lobotomy.

Moniz didn't invent the lobotomy, but he did look at case studies of dead and "pacified" (read: *gorked*) patients from the late 1800s and think "that seems like a good idea!" Even for the experimental science of the 1930s, the practice seems so cruel and short-sighted that it would make any sane person wonder whether Moniz should have been the one being lobotomized. Instead, remarkably, the scientific community rewarded him with a Nobel Prize for Physiology or Medicine for his stab-and-cut method of surgical, empathy-free mental-health therapy. But today, Moniz's contribution to science is making therapy apps seem like a useful option.

Re: Eternal Damnation

```
Let's give Antonio the modern equivalent of the
lobotomy: the equally brain-destroying activity of
reading the entire Twilight series and having to attend
a never-ending book club to discuss it.
```

—Satan

RICHARD O. MARSHALL AND EARL R. KOOI

for Being Corny

Some killers use knives. Others use guns. But the real smooth operators use the food we eat every day and get rich doing it, like biochemists Richard O. Marshall and Earl R. Kooi did. They produced an ingredient so terrible for us and so ubiquitous that it may be responsible for millions of lives lost (to both death and the siren song of the couch): high-fructose corn syrup.

One of the many plant-based caloric sweeteners that hide in plain sight in lists of unpronounceable ingredients, HFCS is worse even than cane sugar. That delicious (and socially acceptable) white powder may make some of the most scrumptious things on earth, but let's face it: it's bad for us. It rots our teeth, makes us fat, and contributes to a variety of diseases. HFCS takes things up a notch. It's not just cheaper than sugar, making those toaster pastries extra tempting, it's also so potently sweet that the human body doesn't really know how to process it, storing it as fat and letting it just kind of hang around the bloodstream like a slow-acting poison. And it's been doing it since the 1970s, thanks to Marshall and Kooi and the Corn Products Refining Company. Did they know they'd be responsible for skyrocketing obesity and diabetes rates? Probably not. But as the saying goes, "The road to Hell is paved with good intentions."

Re: Eternal Damnation

Richard and Earl should enjoy the fruits of their labor—all the foods filled with their HFCS, all the time, so that they feel as bloated and useless as their living countrymen do.

—Satan

THE PEOPLE YOU MEET IN HELL

METER MAID

★★★☆☆
for Total Indifference

Of all the most absurd ways to earn a living, meter maid has to be somewhere near the top. Oh, you're thirty-five seconds past due for that parking space? Here's a $100 ticket. Half an inch too far from that curb? Another $100 ticket. What in the name of micromanaging nonsense is the point? It's not lost revenue—that parking space costs $10 a day. So ticketing means the towns and companies that own the lots are making a mint off people who had to stop and use the bathroom on their way back to their car. And it's not safety—otherwise, these mall-cop rejects would be going after the speeders in souped-up Honda Civics whose obnoxious dual exhaust is the bane of everyone's existence.

Basically paid stalkers, meter maids circle the same spots over and over, all day long, hoping someone slips up. Who hurt you, meter maids? Who gave you those control issues you're clinging to and imposing on innocent tourists and city residents? You think you've earned the title of "parking enforcement officer"? No, meter maid. The only job that could be more of a burr in society's butt is telemarketing (see page 117)— and that's saying something!

Re: Eternal Damnation

```
Meter maids get to live their afterlife as they see fit,
but they'll be followed around Hell by micromanaging
minor demons who ticket and punish them for every
minor infraction, from leaving the cap off the
toothpaste to chewing too loudly.
```

—Satan

CULT CLASSICS

CHAPTER

3

Thug Behram

for Notoriety

"THIS MAN WAS A PERFECT MASTER OF HIS PROFESSION."

—WILLIAM HENRY SLEEMAN, BRITISH OFFICER AND FANBOY

There was a time when "Thug" might have made it into the baby books as a strong first name. But then Thug Behram came along and ruined it for everyone, making Thug as synonymous with "criminal lowlife" as Karen is with "entitled white lady." And the word's troublesome meaning today is nothing compared with its murderous origins. Behram wasn't just a goon or a hooligan—he had ambition, he had charisma, and he had a talent for strangling people with a handkerchief and a coin, which he expertly pressed against the victim's Adam's apple.

Behram was a shy little boy in late-1700s India until a practiced criminal took him under his wing. By the age of twenty-five, he was routinely killing people on the street in India's Oudh region and stealing their money. (It's always the quiet ones.) At the time, the British were doing a good amount of subjugating and exploiting Indians. Behram simply dished out more than he took. He formed a movement—or, more accurately, a gang—of anti-colonists called Thugees who would disguise themselves as British soldiers and pilgrims. When everyone went to sleep, they made sure more than a few didn't wake up. In all, Behram and his thugs are said to have killed 931 people—a Guinness world record!—by the time he was hanged at the ripe old age of seventy-five.

Re: Eternal Damnation

Hugs, not thugs! He'll get them forever—bone-crushing ones, from me personally.

—Satan

Hong Xiuquan

★☆☆☆☆
for Omnipotence

Usually when someone fails multiple civil-service tests, has a mental breakdown, and starts seeing visions, they get some rest, some therapy, and maybe a vacation. They don't lead a country-wide rebellion. Not Hong Xiuquan. The Christian convert convinced himself that his failures and delusions were all part of a greater plan to save China, centered around him being the second son of God. Amazingly, he was not immediately ushered into his very own padded room. Instead, he found his audience—vast numbers of peasants struggling to get by under the Qing Dynasty. They needed a savior, and Hong selflessly offered his services.

Preaching equality and justice, Hong led his followers in a revolt against the government. (It's probably a total coincidence that this was the same government he had tried desperately and failed to join—four times.) The Taiping Rebellion initially worked, possibly because the defensive troops were high on opium, but also because the rebels' ranks swelled to more than a million zealots ready to leave it all on the field for Hong's Heavenly Kingdom of Great Peace. But then European armies arrived to quell the uprising, and things went downhill. Hong's stress-induced utopic vision turned into a fourteen-year civil war that killed as many as 20 million people. In retrospect, therapy was probably the better option.

Re: Eternal Damnation

They say, "be careful what you wish for." All this type-A guy really wanted was to work in government, so let's make it happen. He can spend eternity navigating the red tape of Hell's DMV.

—Satan

THE PEOPLE YOU MEET IN HELL

PUBLIC RESTROOM OFFENDER

★★☆☆☆
for Bad Streaming Content

Theoretically, pretty much all adults have been potty-trained. But too many of those people seem to forget how to properly use a toilet when in a public place. Somehow, just knowing that some unfortunate and underpaid stranger will clean up after them makes them unable to do anything correctly or maintain even the lowest possible semblance of human decency. They leave urine (or much, much worse) on the seat, rim, floor, handle, and—inexplicably—wall, and then they have the audacity not to flush. Apparently, they believe "if it's yellow, let it mellow," and also "if it's brown, let it stick around." Don't pretend it's about not wanting to touch that bacteria-covered handle—we see you leaving without washing your hands. Shame! Shame on you for doing in a public bathroom what you would never do in your own home for fear of having to clean up your own mess. The person who has to use that stall after you should get to tie you to a post and spray you with a cold garden hose like a dog that's rolled in muck.

Re: Eternal Damnation

Anyone caught consistently leaving public bathrooms worse than they found them gets to clean the porta-potties after Hell's monthly Extra-Spicy Chili Cookoff and Watery Beer Drinking Contest.

—Satan

Nathan Bedford Forrest

> "GET THERE FIRST WITH THE MOST MEN."
>
> —NATHANIEL BEDFORD FORREST, TACTICAL GENIUS

for Pride

Smarting over their loss in the Civil War—which they convinced themselves was about "states' rights" and not "the right for rich people to own other people and force them to work their cotton plantations"—a bunch of frustrated Confederate soldiers got together in Pulaski, Tennessee, on Christmas Eve 1865. But they didn't go for eggnog, camaraderie, and midnight Mass. These petty losers decided to form a hate group to whine about and take back the power they felt they were entitled to simply because they were white guys. Their leader and the KKK's first Grand Wizard: Nathan Bedford Forrest.

That makes perfect sense when you realize Forrest also led the Fort Pillow Massacre in April 1864, in which he and his men brutally attacked a primarily Black regiment, many members of which were attempting to surrender when they were killed. But Forrest had skin in the game—literally, he made his money as a slave trader—and didn't want to lose it. (Tough break, buddy.) Being a white guy with big feelings, he decided to take his frustration out on a large group of human beings who did absolutely nothing to him, which tracks. Little did Forrest know that he would spawn generations of hateful, stupid dudes flying Confederate flags from rusty pickup trucks. (And, like Forrest, they will probably also die from uncontrolled diabetes.) He'd be so proud.

Re: Eternal Damnation

He came with his own hood? Let's make it airtight and pipe in every fart the famously flatulent Hitler ever passed. Shallow breaths, Nate!

—Satan

THE PEOPLE YOU MEET IN HELL

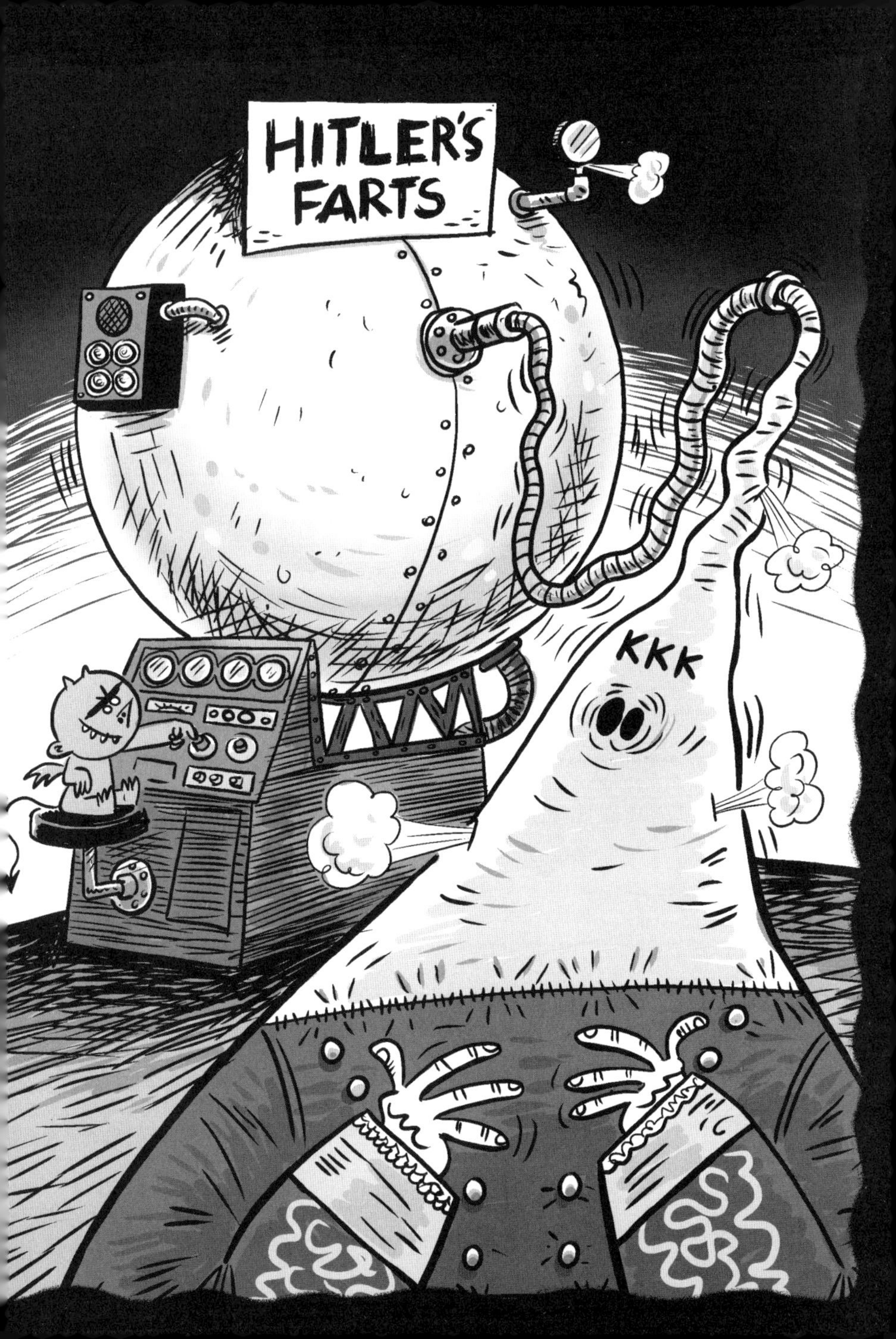
HITLER'S FARTS
KKK

JOSEPH STALIN

★★★★★
for Purging

After the death of Vladimir Lenin in 1924, the fight for control of the Soviet Union and the great communist experiment came down to two acolytes: Leon Trotsky and Joseph Stalin. Stalin emerged as the leader early on, but it didn't stop him from continuing to shove Trotsky aside to keep hold of that and Stalin shoved hard—first by having Trotsky exiled to a remote part of Soviet Central Asia in 1928 and eventually *having Trotsky killed via ice pick.* If you think that might be a harbinger of things to come, you'd be right!

Trotsky's assassination wasn't Stalin's first or last murderous rodeo. Driven by the usual toxic-narcissist cocktail of fear, paranoia, and resentment, he had a habit of killing or imprisoning his enemies—real and perceived. Once in office, he purged the government of them through both your garden-variety violence and showy kangaroo courts, the inevitable result of which was being shuffled off to the Gulag or to work camps in freezing Siberia. His Great Purge of so-called enemies of the state resulted in the execution of hundreds of thousands more, including many high-ranking government and military officials. And that's not counting all the deaths his terrible policies caused. All in all, the vicious dictator's body count is estimated in the millions. But hey, at least he got some cool statues out of it.

Re: Eternal Damnation

Joey thinks running a government is scary? Stick him in Hell's premier haunted house, full of endless twists, turns, and tortures. That'll keep his head on a swivel!

—Satan

THE PEOPLE YOU MEET IN HELL

BENITO MUSSOLINI

★★★★☆
for Fascism

"WE BECOME STRONGEST, I FEEL,
WHEN WE HAVE NO FRIENDS
UPON WHOM TO LEAN, OR TO LOOK
FOR MORAL GUIDANCE."

—BENITO MUSSOLINI, PINPOINTING THE PROBLEM

If you want something done right, you have to do it yourself. Maybe that's why Benito Mussolini founded Italian fascism in 1919, seized the role of prime minister in 1922, and promoted himself to absolute ruler in 1925. And King Victor Emmanuel III kindly rolled out the red carpet for them, allowing Mussolini to form his own government. Calling himself *Il Duce* ("the leader"), Mussolini immediately started passing laws to give himself greater control before finally outing himself as the violent dictator he really was.

But Mussolini didn't do things right so much as he led his country into three consecutive wars, the third of which got him ousted. (Apparently, Italians lived by a three-strike rule.) When World War II broke out, Mussolini allowed Nazis to run ragged over Europe in exchange for Hitler staying out of the way of his land grabs elsewhere. Eventually, though, his countrymen got sick of losing, and the king relieved Mussolini of his duties. (Ouch.) Rightfully fearing retribution for years of dictatorship, Mussolini bolted. His good friend the Führer put him in charge of German-occupied northern Italy, where he killed thousands of Italian Jews before being found full of bullets himself and hung upside down like a morbid piñata for all to enjoy.

Re: Eternal Damnation

Benny must have missed those kindergarten lessons in patience and not taking what doesn't belong to you. For not playing nice, he'll be the designated placeholder in theme-park lines for better people, always waiting but never reaping the rewards.

—Satan

ADOLF HITLER

★★★★★
for Audacity

"WHAT LUCK FOR RULERS THAT MEN DO NOT THINK."

—ADOLF HITLER, INSPIRING GENERATIONS OF POLITICIANS

Where do we even start with Adolf "Napoleon, but Also a Serial Killing Monster with a Bad Mustache" Hitler? To say that "Hitler" is synonymous with "loathsome," "hateful," "evil incarnate," and "the most irredeemable human who ever lived" would be an understatement. With an ego so big that there wasn't any room for humility, doubt, or even an ounce of common sense, the megalomaniac set out to conquer all of Europe by violent force. And he got unbelievably far for a vegetarian with a weak stomach.

Hitler's rise to power was the perfect storm: a population burned out by war and slowly groomed by hateful propaganda mixed with a fragile white guy who'd been rejected by art school . . . twice. And it resulted in the deaths of millions of people, most of whom were Jewish. Why? Because Hitler decided that Jews, who made up 500,000 of Germany's 67 million residents—or 0.75 percent—were to blame for all the country's problems. (Clearly, he was as good at math and deductive reasoning as he was at art.) Then, when defeat was imminent, the coward took his own life while his cousin-bride snacked on cyanide. A full eighty years later, this guy is still bringing out the worst in people. Heck of a legacy!

Re: Eternal Damnation

This insult to the memory of Charlie Chaplin's mustache can spend his afterlife having each hair of his plucked out, slowly and painfully, while listening to Yiddish music. L'chaim, buddy!

—Satan

MAO TSE-TUNG

for A Great Leap Backward

If you grew up in the US during the twentieth century, you probably heard wild tales about how the "all for one and one for all" system of socialism would send American society plunging into chaos, starvation, ineptitude, and cannibalism. And the people angrily telling those tales usually pointed to China's communist policies as proof. So really, we have Mao Tse-tung (as well as Americans' inability to understand the difference) to thank for the horrific state of our social safety nets.

A self-styled political prophet and cult figure, Chairman Mao created his 1958 Frankenstein policy from the beliefs of Marx, Lenin, and Stalin—three guys you definitely want to emulate (*insert eye roll here*). His goal was to show its superiority compared to Western capitalism, but China suffered unimaginably under his ambitious but disastrous reign. Mao essentially tried to make an eighty-year shift from agriculture to industry happen in fifteen years by, among other idiotic things, forcing people to switch from farming to forging steel. Nobody knew what they were doing, the country ran out of coal, and there wasn't enough food to feed its 700 million people. Whatever they did produce was shipped overseas to make it look like Mao's plan was working. People who hoarded food and didn't share were killed, which made some resort to cannibalism. In the end, Mao's "Great Leap Forward" cost his country more than 45 million lives over four years. Solid plan!

Re: Eternal Damnation

Mao likes messing with things that work? He should love experiencing Daylight Savings Time every week for eternity—and all the sluggishness and disorientation that comes with it.

—**Satan**

THE PEOPLE YOU MEET IN HELL

DAVID BERG

★☆☆☆☆
for **Disgracing Hippies**

"HEAVEN IS HERE TO STAY, AND SEX IS HERE TO STAY!"

—DAVID BERG, FORWARD THINKER

Sexual freedom was big in the 1960s, but even the hippies promoting their defiantly progressive message of free love in opposition to the bloody quagmire that was the Vietnam War had their limits. In 1968, religious guy David Berg used the messaging of their movement to create a cult that did not share those limits. First named the icky and obviously predatory Teens for Christ and later the Children of God, Berg's "church" encouraged free love between family members, children, and total strangers in the name of Christ—a pedophilia ring for the Lord. He also advocated "flirty fishing" to his followers, telling his young, female followers to essentially prostitute themselves and seduce influential and wealthy men into the church.

Once the cult was in the crosshairs of legal authorities the world over (for obvious reasons), David Berg went into hiding and renamed his church "The Family." He still managed to deliver thousands of missives to his followers and messages to the public—usually rants about how mainstream religions, the government, and laws that prevented him from having sex with children were evil. Normal cult-leader stuff. Berg died in Portugal in 1994, still gracing most-wanted lists, but The Family (now rebranded as The Family International) persists with his widow at the helm. (She claims to have done away with all the incest, pedophilia, and prostitution, though. So that's something.)

Re: Eternal Damnation

Since Dave's a big fan of teens, he can be one forever, subject to the hormones, acne, awkwardness, and whatever inane trend the teens are into at each moment.

—Satan

ERVIL LEBARON

for Creative Justification

> "I HAVE NOT DONE ANYTHING
> CONTRARY TO WHAT GOD
> HAS TOLD ME TO DO."
>
> —ERVIL LEBARON, POINTING A RATHER
> LARGE FINGER

Despite values of kindness and serenity, the Mormon church has a pretty messy history involving grandiose leaders, murderous mobs, and memorable massacres. Ervil LeBaron kept that tradition going strong in the late twentieth century, when the church was desperately trying to put all of that behind them. (But with a name like a villainous cartoon weasel in a fedora, what do you expect?)

LeBaron left what was already a cultish offshoot of the church in 1972, after he was unable to wrestle control of it from his brother or successfully order his assassination. He started his own sect of that sect: the Church of the Lamb of God, which operated alongside drug cartels out of Chihuahua, Mexico. LeBaron claimed to speak directly with God, who supposedly told him that he could use a discredited Mormon tenet called "blood atonement" to cleanse the evil out of others (aka execute them and let them bleed out on the ground). LeBaron somehow managed to amass hundreds of followers—not to mention thirteen wives and fifty-one children—who were all good with that and carried out as many as fifty "God-ordained" murders (and many other crimes) on his behalf. And they kept going long after he was arrested in Mexico, extradited to the US, and jailed for life, where he died in 1981.

Re: Eternal Damnation

What's in a name? In Ervil's case, a foretelling resemblance to the word "evil." But also, a tank of a classic vehicle. He'll wander Hell's version of the Mexican desert, pursued by a possessed Chrysler LeBaron that's gunning for him.

—Satan

THE PEOPLE YOU MEET IN HELL

CLOSE TALKER

★★★☆☆

for Space Invasion

First of all, why are you even talking to me, close talker? You could have texted, or waved from across the room, or—better yet—gone about your day without involving another person at all. You corner the helpless store clerk or the hapless stranger and lean all the way in until they can tell what you had for dinner two nights ago—and it invariably involved onions, garlic, and a complete lack of mouthwash. It's like being talked at in 4D with smell-o-vision. You invade their little bubble of personal and mental space, offending them with your smell and closeness at the best of times. And these are far from the best of times. In the age of viruses whipping their way through a reckless public, it's an act of violence to get this close to another person just to tell them your boring bruised-avocado story. And I'm not going to listen to what you're saying anyway because I'm annoyed, enraged, and sickened by your passive-aggressively predatory behavior and your need to trap another person into spending time with you. Instead, you need to spend some time in a quiet room by yourself and reflect on your choices, because something is clearly missing from your life. And it's not me. Do the work; respect the bubble.

Re: Eternal Damnation

For the close talkers, Hell is not other people. Hell is a silent meditation retreat in a remote location with their very own yurt and no neighbors for miles. Try close-talking with the wildlife and see how that goes.

—Satan

Pol Pot

for Insecurity

There's nothing like taking away people's rights, money, religion, and property and demanding they conform to your political views to make them love you. You would think the outcry, the poverty, and the death might make that leader pump the breaks, but dictators seem to prefer a Grand Theft Auto approach to reform. Pol Pot, for example, looked at the bleakness and failures of twentieth-century communist movements in China and thought, "Hold my beer."

Pot's early years were a mixed bag of mediocre grades, trade school, and study abroad. He got a taste for politics, specifically communism, in Paris. But Pot wanted none of that wimpy, pseudo-capitalist communism. In 1975, Pot and his Khmer Rouge—a party dedicated to enacting pure Marxism in Cambodia—remade the country into their own socialist utopia. But instead of helping people, they caused about a million deaths. One of Pot's biggest triggers was intellectualism. If you had a degree, wore glasses, spoke more than one language, or in any way seemed too smart to conform, you were tortured, executed, or forced to work yourself to death in the "killing fields." (Considering Pot flunked out of school multiple times, that feels personal.) Thankfully, an invasion by Vietnam in 1979 sent Pot into hiding and the Khmer Rouge spiraling until it finally fizzled out almost twenty years later.

Re: Eternal Damnation

Time for school! The classes will keep repeating, but Pol will never get those grades up. And after school, he'll spend hours writing "I will not kill people who are smarter than me" on the blackboard.

—Satan

FRED PHELPS

★★★★☆
for Exhibitionism

"YOU'RE NOT GOING TO GET
NOWHERE WITH THAT SLOP THAT
'GOD LOVES YOU.'"

—FRED PHELPS, PREACHER

Talk about a vocal minority—Fred Phelps was disbarred by his own colleagues, disavowed by his religion, and disowned by (some of) his kids for his bizarre and hateful protests against "sinfulness" (aka people minding their own business). No one knows what snapped in Fred Phelps's brain to make the former civil rights attorney crudely and abominably trash the LGBTQ+ community and its allies at every turn. But he founded the Westboro Baptist Church in 1955 to do just that. It bore pretty much no resemblance to a Baptist organization or a church but was more of an outlet for Phelps's rage-fueled narcissism. This guy had the PR instincts of a Kardashian, and he'd do anything to get in front of a camera.

Phelps's claim to infamy was trotting out his prodigious commune-dwelling brood to make it seem like he had followers and protesting funerals, of all things. They made the most headlines by "celebrating" the funerals of fallen American military personnel—not because they were gay, but because they fought for a country that (just barely) tolerated homosexuality. And despite complaints about offensive language when he was a fledgling evangelical, Phelps didn't seem to mind using it himself to catch the media's attention and tout his firm belief that God hates human beings. Great guy. Super chill.

Re: Eternal Damnation

It turns out God doesn't hate everyone. He just hates Fred. And he's asked me to sentence him to an eternity of *Will and Grace* reruns.

—Satan

JIM JONES

★★★☆☆
for Hitting His Quota

> "I'D LIKE TO CHOOSE MY OWN KIND OF DEATH, FOR A CHANGE. I'M TIRED OF BEING TORMENTED TO HELL. TIRED OF IT."
>
> —JIM JONES, IRONICALLY

Jim Jones wasn't the first to proclaim himself a Messiah. He's just the one who wore ridiculous far-from-*Top Gun* shades, rocked a LEGO Minifigure hairdo, and convinced his followers to drink cyanide-laced Flavor Aid. Yep, the guy was too cheap to go for the name-brand stuff—even for his big mass suicide.

This paranoid, needy egomaniac, who liked to be called "The Prophet," brought his eager Peoples Temple followers from California to a vanity project—that he called Jonestown (did we mention he was an egomaniac?)—in the jungles of Guyana. And once they were onto his con, he used blackmail, beatings, and death threats to keep them there. (They probably should have taken their chances.)

Fearful that the authorities were after him—and they were—Jones made his adherents rehearse mass suicides. And after his lieutenants murdered a sitting US congressman who was leading an investigation into the cult, Jones ordered the self-takeout for real. He forced more than 900 people to "drink the Kool-Aid," leaving behind only a handful of survivors and one of the most tired phrases in the contemporary vernacular.

Re: Eternal Damnation

You know the old Kool-Aid ads, where the sentient glass pitcher full of red dye #40 bursts through a brick wall and shouts, "Oh, yeah!"? Jim shall forever find himself on the other side of that wall. *Oh, no!*

—Satan

CHARLES MANSON

★★★★★
for Delegating

A madman, a cult leader, and a mass murderer, Charles Manson hit a rare trifecta of earthbound evil. Manson was a small-time criminal and misogynist turned charismatic leader who orchestrated violent acts of murder via his starry- (and glassy-) eyed followers in hopes of starting a race war. He called his doomsday prediction "Helter Skelter," bastardizing the title of a really great Beatles song (yet another unforgivable act).

Manson embraced the hippies' whole long-haired, unshaven, guitarist-with-a-dream vibe, and it worked for him. He had a knack for hypnotizing young, abused, runaway women into doing what he wanted. But rather than espousing the "free love" mantra of the '60s, this waste of good hair provided a not-so-peaceful counter to the counterculture. Claiming he was Jesus (among other things), Manson got his "family" to commit more than thirty-five murders for his racist cause. His Unholiness wasn't above petty vendettas, though. Those horrible Sharon Tate murders in 1969? A case of mistaken address. Manson had meant to sic his cult on a music producer who rejected him, but the man had moved. (That's just bad staff work.) But they were already dressed for murder, so . . . . Thankfully, Manson and his minions got jail time, where he would continue putting his crazy on full display for forty years.

Re: Eternal Damnation

The best way to torture a Beatles fan? Force them to listen to Yoko Ono dis the band and perform her own music. Enjoy, Charlie!

—Satan

THE PEOPLE YOU MEET IN HELL

SHOKO ASAHARA

★★★★☆
for Some Grand Delusions

There are two kinds of cult leaders: the ones who abuse and exploit their own loyal followers before getting them killed, and the ones who strike out at the general public, murdering uninvolved innocents. The latter is definitely more evil, making Shoko Asahara, leader of the Japanese "doomsday cult" Aum Shinrikyo and chemical- and biological-weapon enthusiast, a shoo-in for the top twenty worst humans in history.

Asahara was a childhood bully, stealing money and exacting beatings (a living argument that people don't really mature as they grow up). He graduated to selling unregulated pharmaceuticals before getting really into esoteric religions. He mixed up Eastern and Western philosophies until he decided on a combination palatable enough to get him official religion status, publishing deals, and tons of followers. Then, in 1992, he went full crazy and announced he was Jesus reincarnated and could absorb sin and give his magical powers to others. He also claimed there was a worldwide conspiracy involving other faiths and the English royal family. The solution? A nuclear apocalypse, of course. So, naturally, he tried to bring it about by staging terrorist attacks. In 1995, he had his followers release sarin gas on a crowded Tokyo subway, killing thirteen people and injuring 5,500 more. Thankfully, that ensured Asahara and his cult would meet its own implosive end.

Re: Eternal Damnation

Let's see Asahara try his game on the New York City subway in the face of disillusioned locals, crazies, buskers, beggars, toenail clippers, rats, grime, unintelligible announcements, and an ever-changing schedule that makes no sense. He lives there now.

—Satan

THE PEOPLE YOU MEET IN HELL

Slow Walker

★★★★★
for Obstruction

How do they do it? How do they walk so slow, unbothered by the flow of regular foot traffic around them and indifferent to the suffering of the people stuck behind them? It's amazing these people ever get anything done at their insufferable, sloth-like pace. And they seem to take up so much space that no one can get around them no matter how they try, leaving stress, annoyance, and tardiness in their literal wake. Is it arrogance? Or maybe a Zen-like concentration on their own meandering that makes them completely unaware of the huffing and shuffling behind them? Or is it a control thing? *They* have to be in front and set the pace for the rest of humanity while also taking up as much physical space as possible as a way to wrest from the universe some small semblance of power over their lives? If that's the case, it's time for some therapy, buddy. Or maybe a hobby. Hold the fate of some unsuspecting succulent in your hands instead of making an already annoying commute or errand even more tedious. Whether it's a complete lack of self-awareness or of compassion, slow walking is unforgivable.

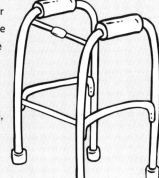

Re: Eternal Damnation

Slow walkers are free to leave Hell whenever they want—as long as they can get around this extremely slow and never-ending parade full of elderly Shriners and marching bands.

—Satan

Osama Bin Laden

> **"AS A MUSLIM, I TRY MY BEST TO AVOID TELLING A LIE."**
>
> —OSAMA BIN LADEN, MID-LIE

★★★★★
for Inviting Chaos

The poster boy for terrorism; the guy whose ugly picture is next to dictionary entries for "evil," "zealot," or even "bad guy"; the twenty-first century bogeyman and turncoat—Osama Bin Laden needs no introduction. If you don't know any other terrorists, you know this guy. Like soccer players and Pele, or architects and Frank Lloyd Wright, he's a leader in his field of the most despicable humans ever to walk the earth.

In 1979, American forces spent a billion dollars on weapons and training to expel the Soviet Union's forces from the Middle East. Who could have guessed that standing between these two powers like a bartender between drunks would get messy? (Other than every person who does not work in government.) The rest is horrifying history: Bin Laden and his mujahideen resistance turned toxic, becoming the fundamentalist, anti-Western, Al Qaeda terrorist organization we all know and hate. Their new goal was to restore fundamental rule (aka fear and misogyny) to the region. With money, followers, and government support behind him, Bin Laden orchestrated a number of terrorist attacks, chiefly the coordinated terrorist attacks on 9/11, which killed nearly 3,000 people. That, *of course*, brought death and destruction down on the Middle East sixty times over. And now we all have to take off our shoes at the airport. Great plan, guy.

Re: Eternal Damnation

The man who made air travel a horrendous ordeal will be subject to never-ending delays, scans, and cavity searches. Don't forget the cavity searches!

—Satan

DAVID KORESH

★★★☆☆
for the Long Con

"IF SOMEONE WANTS TO KILL ME, THEY CAN DO IT. I'M NOT GOING TO RESIST."

—DAVID KORESH, WHILE ARMED TO THE TEETH

Born Vernon Howell, future cult leader David Koresh was a high-school dropout with a guitar who was searching for a purpose. He tried the church, but he was thrown out for being a bad influence. After heading to Hollywood and failing to become a rock star in the late 1970s—a time when they were letting pretty much anybody be rock stars, including that "Piña Colada Song" guy—in 1981 Koresh joined a religious cult in Waco, Texas, called the Branch Davidians. And since he couldn't be the next Kurt Cobain, he became the next Jim Jones (see page 107).

Twenty-two-year-old Koresh started out by romancing the cult's sixty-something prophetess. When she died, he tussled with her son for power. But since he had a handful of zealots and a whole lot of automatic weapons, he won. Koresh settled into the Branch Davidians' Waco compound, changed his name ("for publicity and business purposes"), and told everyone that God wanted their wives and preteen daughters to sleep with him (among other crazy things). Not wanting another Jonestown situation on their hands, the government eventually invaded the compound. But they accidentally brought the cyanide themselves, in the form of tear gas that caught fire and killed almost everyone, including Koresh. It's cool, though, because there are still some survivors hanging out in Waco, waiting for their cult brethren to rise from the dead.

Re: Eternal Damnation

Attention-seeking much? Dave can play Hell's worst dive bar, where he'll be heckled and have to either dodge rotting fruit or be completely ignored.

—Satan

THE PEOPLE YOU MEET IN HELL

ADOLFO CONSTANZO

for Loyalty

> "DEATH IS ONLY A TRANSITION TO A DIFFERENT FORM OF EXISTENCE. IT'S NOTHING TO BE AFRAID OF."
>
> —ADOLFO CONSTANZO, GUY CAUSING THE DEATH

Leading a Satanic cult *as well as* a drug-trafficking ring? Adolfo "The Godfather" Constanzo was the peanut-butter cup of frightening criminals, combining two great tastes that taste great together. (Well, maybe not so much for his victims or the people of northeastern Mexico who risked stumbling across their dismembered remains every time they left the house.)

In the 1980s, Constanzo led the so-called Narcosatanists cult, which used black magic and believed they'd win greater favor from their dark lord with a series of live human sacrifices. Constanzo and company killed and mutilated at least twenty-seven people, leaving the remains just lying around in Mexico City. But as anyone who's been to a new-age store can tell you, magical accoutrement is expensive. Cocaine was the group's side hustle and funded the whole endeavor. It was a great combo until it came back to bite them. In search of a victim, they kidnapped and killed American student Mark Kilroy instead of the usual prostitute or drug dealer. Authorities turned up the heat. And on April 1, 1989, a member of the cult drove through a police barricade and led the police straight to the ranch. Why? Because he thought he was invisible. Because magic. But Constanzo had the last laugh—sort of. He asked a follower to kill him, thus *magically* eluding capture.

Re: Eternal Damnation

Adolfo would make a great assistant to Hell's resident magician, Daemon the Magnificent, whose torturous talent is being the worst magician in all the realms. (Don't get too attached to those doves, buddy.)

—Satan

MOHAMMED YUSUF

★★★★☆
for Diehard Beliefs

If nothing else, at least Mohammed Yusuf died doing what he loved—fighting in an extremely violent uprising started by the followers of the dangerous organization he founded. OK, he died *just after* fighting, while in police custody. Close enough. But his archaic and anarchistic ideas lived on while many, many other people did not because of them, and that's what really counts.

Yusuf started Boko Haram in Nigeria just seven years earlier, in 2002. It was equal parts religious cult, paramilitary group, terrorist organization, and radical political movement because Yusuf himself was a fundamentalist (OK, a zealot . . . OK, a terrorist) who believed in a radical reading of ancient Muslim scriptures. He even publicly rejected scientific facts that conflicted with his spiritual beliefs, including that the earth is round and that condensation causes rain. And he so wanted that interpretation to be the law of the world that he was willing to kill over it. Whether he or not he was willing to die for it is another matter, but die he did, in a clash between Boko Haram and the Nigerian military that killed more than 1,000 people. It turns out that, like any middle manager, Yusuf wasn't all that essential to his organization. His followers continued to routinely kidnap and torture large groups of people in the name of Allah. Thanks to Yusuf's bright ideas, Boko Haram has killed more than 35,000 people in its quest for world domination and capitulation. Gotta love a fundamentalist!

Re: Eternal Damnation

The CEO of Bad Ideas can be part of endless brainstorming meetings—in person, first thing in the morning every day, and at 4:59 on Fridays.

—Satan

THE PEOPLE YOU MEET IN HELL

TELEMARKETER

★★★★★
for Sheer Desperation

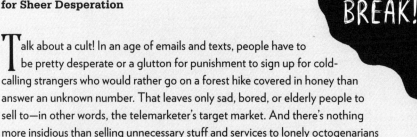

Talk about a cult! In an age of emails and texts, people have to be pretty desperate or a glutton for punishment to sign up for cold-calling strangers who would rather go on a forest hike covered in honey than answer an unknown number. That leaves only sad, bored, or elderly people to sell to—in other words, the telemarketer's target market. And there's nothing more insidious than selling unnecessary stuff and services to lonely octogenarians on a fixed income.

Anyone who lasts more than two weeks in the job has to be dead inside, completely indifferent to the annoyance of others, to harass the public at large with endless calls about extended car warranties and life insurance plans. You ignore their calls? Try ignoring one every hour. You block their number? They just spoof a new one. Whether they're hawking legitimate products or trying to scam you into sharing your Social Security number with the whole of the dark web, telemarketers are the bottom-feeders of society, a blight on a communications industry that has come so far. If you want to market unneces-sary garbage to the masses, you should get with the times and let Google do the harassing for you.

Re: Eternal Damnation

```
Telemarketing is its own punishment, which is why
people who choose to do it on Earth get stuck doing it
in Hell. (We're always looking for good telemarketers
down here.)
```

—Satan

MURDERERS
MOST FOUL

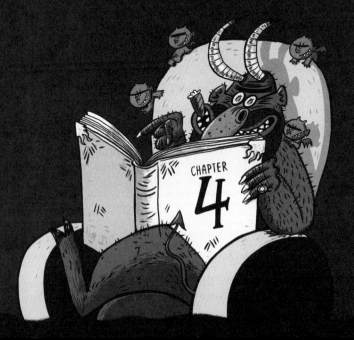

MARY ANN COTTON

★★★★★
for Marrying Wisely

In the nineteenth century, people just didn't have the variety of poisons at their disposal like they do today. If you wanted to kill someone, you had to make do with what you had. And for Mary Ann Cotton and every other murderer in Victorian England, that was arsenic—a substance so ubiquitous that her lawyer argued that her victims died from dusty arsenic-dyed wallpaper.

Before the era of identification and tracking that she probably helped inspire, Cotton had a nasty habit of meeting a guy, marrying him, popping out some kids, and then killing the whole lot of them using mommy's toxic little helper. She'd cash the insurance payout, move to a new town, and do it all over again. Only once did a husband (husband number three, that is) get suspicious, and, by then, she'd already killed two of his kids and one of her own. (If Cinderella had known about Cotton, she'd have thanked her lucky stars for her stepmother's run-of-the-mill cruelty.) But she just moved on and did it again with husband number four, who didn't catch on quickly enough. After killing twenty-one people between 1852 and 1873, a suspicious official finally ordered autopsies and exhumations. Authorities found huge levels of arsenic in multiple bodies and put a ring on it—a noose.

Re: Eternal Damnation

Modern insurance is its own form of torture, and Hell's medical plan changes monthly! Mary Ann will find herself stuck in an infinite and endlessly frustrating loop of trying to find participating providers, meet her deductibles, and file claims online.

–Satan

OBNOXIOUS PICKUP TRUCK DRIVER

for Tailgating

N ot all pickup truck drivers are Hell-bound jerks, but there are an awful lot of Hell-bound jerks who are pickup truck drivers. Being behind the wheel of a larger-than-average vehicle can bring out the aggressive nightmare in some humans. These obnoxious overcompensating nuisances love to tailgate, hands gesticulating angrily, while they swerve in the lane behind you to make sure you know they're not happy about being second in line. Then they pass you with about two inches of space between your vehicles, a loud vroom, a honking of the horn, and a puff of climate-killing exhaust. This gives you just enough time to get a glimpse of the driver's super classy Truck Nutz, aggro bumper stickers, and mirrored shades, so you take a deep breath and try not to flip off an obvious psychopath as they speed away. But, hey, at least they made it to the gas station a whole two minutes before you, so they win! And then they have the audacity to complain to you about high gas prices for their pollution machines, like you're in this together, before pulling up to the convenience store and taking up two spots so they can reload on the energy drinks that fuel their frustrated personalities. Here's a suggestion—try a nice herbal tea next time and maybe you won't end up in the Bad Place.

> **Re: Eternal Damnation**
>
> Anyone who owns and displays Truck Nutz is automatically reincarnated as Truck Nutz. It was written into my contract with their inventor to get the stupid things on the market.
>
> —Satan

JANE TOPPAN

★★★★☆
for Nursing a Dream

"THAT IS MY AMBITION, TO HAVE KILLED MORE PEOPLE—MORE HELPLESS PEOPLE—THAN ANY MAN OR WOMAN WHO HAS EVER LIVED."

—JANE TOPPAN, AN INSPIRATION

Nurses are supposed to help sick people get better, but that was way too much effort for New England nurse Jane Toppan. So she helped her patients skip ahead to the dying part, even if she had to shave a few decades off their lives to do it. This was no empathy-driven Kevorkian-style service she was providing her patients. Toppan got a sexual thrill from watching patients walk toward the light. And it wasn't just patients—she used her medical know-how to off her competition, her foster sister, and pretty much anyone else who bugged her or got in her way.

Despite pretty consistent reports of theft, incompetence, strange behavior, and a disturbing number of healthy people dropping dead around her, doctors kept referring Toppan to wealthy families as one of the best. (Life was a little rougher back in the late 1800s, but come on!) But after she killed four healthy people in a single family, a surviving relative suspected something was amiss. (You think?) He had authorities exhume and autopsy one of the bodies, which showed fatal doses of atropine and morphine. Toppan fessed up to everything, admitting she'd killed at least thirty-one people in similar manners. But, according to her, she was just following her dream . . . which is why she spent the rest of her *natural* life in a mental institution.

Re: Eternal Damnation

Let's make her dreams come true—specifically the weird ones about being covered in snakes, buried alive, or caught mid high school hallway in her underwear.

—Satan

H. H. HOLMES

★★★★★

for Running the Worst Hotel in History

"I COULD NOT HELP THE FACT THAT I WAS A MURDERER, NO MORE THAN A POET CAN HELP THE INSPIRATION TO SING."

—HERMAN MUDGETT, MODESTLY

Everybody needs to shake up their career now and then. Small-time con man Herman Webster Mudgett felt that itch and scratched it harder than a kid with chicken pox, becoming both a part-time renovator and full-time murderer. Just before the 1893 Chicago World's Fair, Mudgett moved to Chicago, changed his name to Dr. H. H. Holmes (who can blame him?), and refurbished a building with secret chutes, tunnels, and trap doors. Then he rented out rooms to visitors who were in town for the fair. Nothing wrong with a side hustle, right? But according to the lore, Mr. Mudgett/Dr. Holmes turned this wholesome HGTV show into *Bates Motel*.

Those who were unlucky enough to snag a spot at the worst Airbnb of all time were killed in their rooms and then conveyed via Holmes's elaborate system to the basement, where he'd incinerate the bodies. By the time he was captured in 1894 (for a separate, horse-related con), he'd killed as many as twenty-seven people. Career-change achievement activated! Today, there's some skepticism surrounding whether Holmes's home had as many murderous bells and whistles as storied. But one thing's for sure: this guy was killing people—lovers, business partners, strangers—like it was his job.

Re: Eternal Damnation

The creator of the "Murder Castle" can spend his afterlife in the exact opposite—a rundown motel, in which he'll be a sentient, stained, and battle-worn mattress. Rest easy there, Herman!

—Satan

ALBERT FISH

★★★★★
for Sheer Depravity

"IT TOOK ME NINE DAYS TO EAT HER ENTIRE BODY."

—ALBERT FISH, INCRIMINATING HIMSELF

He's the serial killer's serial killer, the murderer to whom other murderers aspire, and a man so freaking gaunt he makes Tom Brady look like Peter Griffin—probably due to a diet consisting of people he killed. Albert Fish eluded capture and even identification for years in the 1920s and 1930s. To most, he was a shadowy stick figure known as "The Brooklyn Vampire." But that would turn out to be a misnomer. Fish didn't merely drink his victims' blood—he ate their bodies too.

In a historically great self-own, Fish gave himself away by using branded stationery that authorities were able to easily trace back to him. On it, he penned a long-winded letter to the mother of one young victim in which he *offered up personal details* and recounted how he'd murdered her daughter, including which parts of the girl he most enjoyed eating. (A regular Dean Koontz, this guy.) Although he confessed to only a few gruesome ends, Fish claimed to have murdered and eaten as many as one hundred people.

Cannibalism was just one of the sadomasochist's many kinks. Legend has it that it took two tries to electrocute Fish because he had an inordinate amount of metal in his body—twenty-nine needles in his groin, to be exact, which this human Piercing Pagoda said brought him sexual pleasure. The needle count is accurate, but the execution was all-too-mercifully swift. Looking sharp, Al!

Re: Eternal Damnation

Al's on envelope-stuffing duty for Hell's newsletter. And because cost-cutting measures originated down here, every single one of those cheap envelopes cuts his tongue and mouth. Try eating innocents with a mouth full of paper cuts, Fish!

–Satan

CARL PANZRAM

★★★★★
for Sheer Criminal Volume

"I AM A BUNDLE OF
CONTRADICTIONS."

—CARL PANZRAM, STRAIGHT-UP CRIMINAL

You know that idealized image of the old-timey hobo carrying a bundle on a stick, stealing pies off the windowsills of trusting townsfolk and then moving from town to town by hopping trains? Carl Panzram bludgeoned that innocent archetype to death. He was that hobo riding the rails across the country, but he wasn't harmlessly pilfering baked goods. He was committing theft, arson, rape, and murder every chance he got. Why? Because hurt people hurt people.

After a rougher-than-average childhood, Panzram snapped harder than a Boomer trying to figure out new technology. He was consumed by the need for revenge—but not on the people who'd actually hurt him. No, no, that would make too much sense. Instead, he turned that rage on the unsuspecting public. He continued to commit crimes at home and abroad between jail stints, even robbing the home of William Howard Taft, whose pawned belongings bought him a "murder yacht" that he used to lure young men to their deaths. But he must have worn himself out with all the killing because, by the time he was arrested in Washington, DC, in 1928, he gave officers his real name and confessed to hundreds of rapes and twenty-one murders. Ah, the romance of travel!

Re: Eternal Damnation

Hell is always looking for good travel agents. Carl can make travel plans for us while he spends eternity stuck at his desk in his itchy button-down shirt and tie.

—Satan

LEONARDA CIANCIULLI

"SOAP HAS ALWAYS BEEN MY LIFE'S PASSION."

—LEONARDA CIANCIULLI, UNCLEAR ON THE PROBLEM

for Fighting Death with Death

A mother would do anything for her child—shield them from a bullet, spend hours making their own organic baby food, murder their friends and neighbors in exchange for divine protection—*anything*. OK, that last one might be exclusive to Leonarda Cianciulli, but there were extenuating circumstances. World War II was well underway by 1939, and millions of people were dying in the streets, in concentration camps, and in the fight. So when Cianciulli's son Giuseppe—one of only four surviving children after three miscarriages and ten early deaths—joined the Royal Italian Army, she was understandably concerned. What came next was not quite so easy to understand.

Cianciulli decided that human sacrifice was the only way to keep her son safe, so she lured three innocent neighbors to their deaths with promises of love and jobs. Not only did she fulfill her promise to God, she also turned a profit. Cianciulli had charged each woman a pretty penny for her make-believe services before chopping them up with an axe, turning their bodies into tea cakes and soaps, and selling their belongings. Apparently, her enterprising take on human sacrifice didn't negate its effects, because Giuseppe lived. But despite hiding the evidence in the most cleverly ghoulish way ever, Cianciulli was found out, tried, and jailed.

Re: Eternal Damnation

Let's stick Leonarda in a giant soap bubble that's unpoppable but not impermeable and let her float through Hell, never knowing what torment lies ahead.

—Satan

JACK THE RIPPER

★★☆☆☆
for Humility

Victorian London may have been even filthier and more punishing than Hell, which may be why a serial killer taking people out left and right didn't warrant much fuss. In the last months of 1888, the so-called Jack the Ripper—a pseudonym for a killer never uncovered—viciously murdered at least five women in the squalid Whitechapel neighborhood of London. Sin and violence were commonplace there, but the victims' sex and lower-class status may be most to blame for why they've gone down in history as prostitutes. (If you weren't a man with money, were you really a person to Victorians? No. The answer is no.)

In reality, only one of the victims is confirmed to have been a woman of the night. But all the victims had their throats slit, their organs removed, and their bodies dumped on the street, and that left the public pretty eager to find the culprit. Fortunately for him, police were no match for Jack. And he knew it, which is why he taunted them by dropping notes and dismembered kidneys in the mail. To historians' knowledge, Jack stopped killing after 1892 with about a dozen murders under his belt. But it's pretty hard to say that for sure when you don't know who the guy is.

Re: Eternal Damnation

Scotland Yard may never have identified you, but we know exactly what you did, Jackie Boy. And for that, you'll be spending eternity surrounded by speakers blaring Nickelback songs on repeat.

—Satan

ED GEIN

★ ★ ★ ★ ★
for Upcycling

Artists can find inspiration pretty much anywhere. Just like a delayed train inspired J. K. Rowling to write *Harry Potter*, Ed Gein inspired the creators of three films: *Psycho*, *The Texas Chainsaw Massacre*, and *Silence of the Lambs*. What do those three films have in common? Creepy murderers who used their victims' bodies like props and craft supplies. The films' writers cribbed their villains' whole deal from Gein, an unconventionally creative serial killer active in the 1950s.

Most killers quickly dispose of their victims' bodies, as they're evidence of *murder*, but not Gein. For him, the bodies were the point. He used them for arts and crafts. Gein had a flair for fashion and was totally goth before it was cool. He had skulls (as in actual human skulls) on each of his bedposts, a bowl made out of another skull, masks made from faces, and leggings made from leg skin. Such was Gein's drive to create, to build ghoulish housewares out of the skin and body parts of his victims, that he even supplemented the stash he got through the extremely time-consuming task of murdering and butchering with a little grave robbery. Understandably deemed insane, he spent the remainder of his life eating soft foods that don't require knives in various mental institutions.

Re: Eternal Damnation

I want Eddie taxidermized, dressed in hemp clothing, and displayed like a wax figure in Hell's Museum of Unnatural History. Make sure he's positioned right next to the poison ivy.

—Satan

THE PEOPLE YOU MEET IN HELL

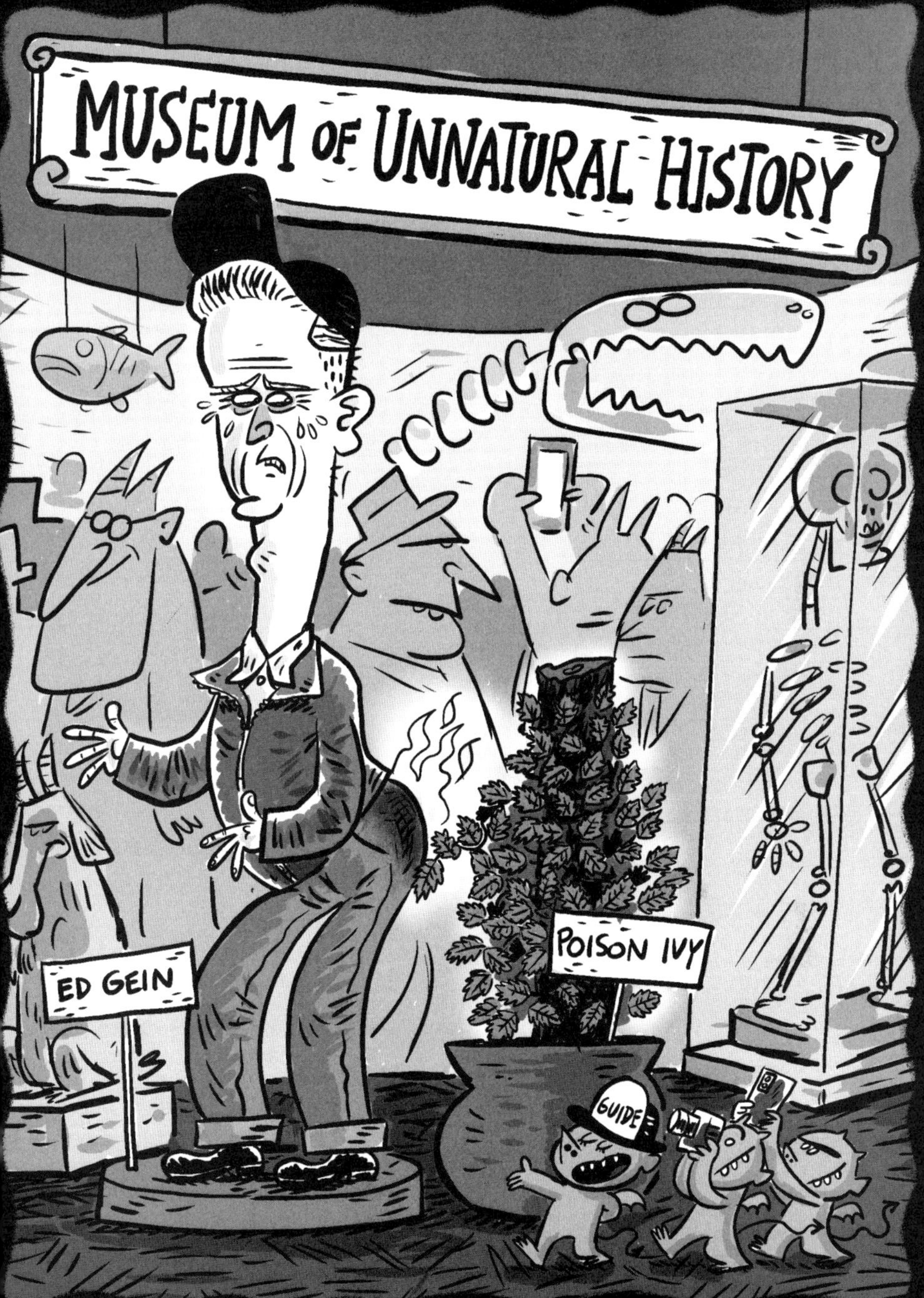
MUSEUM OF UNNATURAL HISTORY
ED GEIN
POISON IVY
GUIDE

LEOPOLD AND LOEB

for Criminal Arrogance

After setting out to commit the perfect crime in 1924, boy geniuses Nathan Leopold and Richard Loeb managed to become two of the world's worst criminals. They'd planned to kidnap, kill, and ransom Loeb's fourteen-year-old cousin Bobby Franks just for the thrill of it. But things didn't go to plan. One blow with the chisel wasn't enough, so their rental car was covered in blood; the hastily disposed of body was discovered before the ransom letter went out; and, most damning of all, Leopold dropped his easily traceable glasses at the scene. (The Wet Bandits from *Home Alone* were criminal masterminds compared to these guys.)

Still, Leopold and Loeb weren't worried—they were rich, young, white men with a good lawyer: the famous Clarence Darrow. But with a mountain of evidence against his clients, Darrow wasn't about to argue innocence. So he argued against the death penalty instead (and got stiffed by Daddy Leopold for his effort). All that privilege got them was life sentences, which is considerably better than the alternative. Loeb died in a razor fight in the prison showers in 1936, but Leopold made it out in 1958, hopefully a little humbler than when he went in.

Re: Eternal Damnation

We've got a lot of geniuses down here. For the duo who think they're so much better than everyone else, let's see how they do in Hell's everlasting Academic Decathlon. My guess is not great.

—Satan

MACK RAY EDWARDS

"I HAVE A GUILT COMPLEX. I COULDN'T EAT, AND I COULDN'T SLEEP, AND IT WAS BEGINNING TO AFFECT MY WORK."

—MACK RAY EDWARDS, RESPONSIBLE EMPLOYEE

★★★★★
for Maintaining Perspective

While few people deserve to lose their lives (outside of everyone listed in this book), there's no greater crime than preying on innocent children. Even the most hardened prisoners, the most depraved lunatics, take exception to messing with kids, imposing more horrifying punishments on the offenders than any criminal-justice system could. That makes Mack Ray Edwards the worst of the worst.

Like a celebrity trying to get ahead of bad press, Edwards turned himself into police when two of his teenage kidnapping victims recognized him and escaped. He admitted to assaulting and killing six children between 1953 and 1970 but later told a Los Angeles County jailer that his true body count was closer to eighteen. Among the dead was his own eleven-year-old sister-in-law, but it still took *surrendering himself* for police to even notice him. Then again, it's tricky when the killer is also a heavy equipment operator for CalTrans and can bury his victims under an ever-expanding freeway system. He dumped the bodies in areas he knew would be paved over. Either the weight of being one of the most horrible humans in history got to Edwards or his cellmates did, because he hanged himself in his cell after a year in the pokey.

Re: Eternal Damnation

Mack deserves to spend eternity driving a beater of a car, alone and stuck in traffic and construction, on a crowded California highway with a radio stuck on NPR.

—Satan

JACK GILBERT GRAHAM

★★★★☆
for Matricide

> "I WATCHED HER GO OFF FOR THE LAST TIME. I FELT HAPPIER THAN I EVER FELT IN MY LIFE."
>
> —JACK GILBERT GRAHAM, STRAIGHT-UP PSYCHO

You think Norman Bates had mommy issues? He had nothing on Jack Gilbert Graham. When this guy decided to off his absentee narcissist of a mom for money, he didn't even flinch at the idea of collateral damage. In 1955, he filled his mother's suitcase with dynamite and programmed it to go off twenty minutes into her flight from Denver to Anchorage. In doing so, he killed forty-three innocent strangers, graduating from murder to mass murder in one fell swooping plane. And he had zero regrets.

Between eyewitnesses and the scent of dynamite hanging in the air, it wasn't hard for investigators to determine foul play was involved. Then they noticed something odd—the plane and all of its inhabitants were in pieces, but all of the luggage was intact. All, that is, except for one customer's: Daisie King. FBI director J. Edgar Hoover (see page 32) instructed the FBI to start taking a closer look at her son, and they soon discovered this wasn't Graham's first rodeo—he'd been convicted of check fraud and bootlegging. He'd even been suspected of trying to blow up his mother's restaurant. Not to mention, he'd hastily taken out several life insurance policies on Mommie Dearest from an airport vending machine. He got the death penalty, obviously.

Re: Eternal Damnation

Jack can spend eternity holed up inside one of our vending machines, where the machinery grabs and pokes at him as Hell's demons order their snacks.

—Satan

THE PEOPLE YOU MEET IN HELL

HENRY LEE LUCAS

★★★★★
for Faking It

"WHAT ARE WE GOING TO DO
ABOUT THESE OTHER HUNDRED
WOMEN I KILLED?"
—HENRY LEE LUCAS, CONCERNED CITIZEN

If ever there was a case study in nurture versus nature, Henry Lee Lucas is it. Raised by abusive alcoholics—including a mom who turned tricks in front of him—Lucas lashed out by molesting siblings and torturing animals as a child. So it's not much of a surprise that he turned out to be an unrepentant serial killer. Or that his first victim was his mom. It's more surprising that her death was the result of a heated argument and not carefully plotted revenge.

Once Lucas slashed his mother's neck in 1969, the murderous barbecue sauce was out of the bottle. He served only ten years of a forty-year sentence, thanks to prison overcrowding, which gave him a chance to meet his soulmate: fellow abused child and convicted killer Ottis Toole. The homely drifter dream team spent the next few years indiscriminately raping, killing, dismembering, and occasionally even eating people across the country—if their stories are to be believed. The duo were definitely serial killers, but reports of their body counts have been greatly exaggerated . . . by them. Lucas alone confessed to six hundred murders, sometimes in startling detail thanks to loose-lipped cops plying him with strawberry milkshakes and cigarettes for his help in closing cases. (Gee, what incentive could he possibly have had to lie?) He was convicted of eleven and died on death row, having led officers on countless wild-goose chases.

Re: Eternal Damnation

Henry's mom has been right here in Hell, waiting for him. Let's put the two of them in a room together and let the torture take care of itself.

—Satan

EVERYDAY
MONSTER
BREAK!

HEAD OF THE HOMEOWNERS' ASSOCIATION

★★★★☆
for Epic Nosiness

Rules, restrictions, and guidelines have their place. Safety regulations in sports? Great. Age restrictions for not-so-healthy habits? Helpful. After all, we need order to protect us from chaos. But decreeing which shade of eggshell you're allowed to paint your house? Only the head of a homeowners' association could come up with something that ridiculous.

These persnickety decoration dictators create arbitrary rules to justify their need for control and enforce them with a dictatorial hand like they're the only things keeping people from devolving into barbarism. This is the hill you've chosen to die on, Susan? To make sure the grass is 1.5 inches and not 1.6 inches long? You don't have anything else to do with your day? It's like a codified version of demanding to speak to the manager, but you are the manager, and of something that doesn't need managing. These guys need to get a life. And if they don't, they can get the afterlife they deserve. Neighborhoods don't need them nosing around people's garbage bins like perpetually annoyed raccoons, and they certainly don't need to be charged $300 a month for the privilege.

Re: Eternal Damnation

So, you like to stay busy? Great. You can spend eternity watching the grass grow past your preferred 1.5 inches and trimming it back. And that house is not quite the right shade of eggshell, Susan. Time to repaint!

–Satan

ANDREI CHIKATILO

★ ★ ★ ★ ★
for Childhood Trauma

From 1978 to 1990—a time when the Soviet Union was at its peak of Cold War hysteria over such horrifying things as Coca-Cola, rock and roll, and blue jeans—actual evil was hiding behind the Iron Curtain. A serial killer, sexual predator, and part-time cannibal named Andrei Chikatilo (aka the Butcher of Rostov, aka the Rostov Ripper) was picking off people left and right. Although police wanted to warn the public about the gruesome murders, the Kremlin chose to keep things quiet. (Much better that their citizens die at the hands of a psychopath than communism take a hit. Stellar governing!)

Between being bullied as a child and teenager, impotent, and a liberal arts major, the odds were stacked against Chikatilo ending up a normal guy. He did have one thing going for him, though—a rare genetic condition that made it impossible (in those days) to match his blood type to the other bodily fluids he so freely left at his crime scenes. When Chikatilo was caught mid-assault with a briefcase full of the usual serial-killer stuff in 1984, police had their suspicions. But without the DNA to back them up, it would take them another six years and a couple dozen more mutilated bodies for authorities to convict him of fifty-two known murders. At least they threw the book at him (i.e., shot him in the head—the USSR didn't play).

Re: Eternal Damnation

Nothing could be worse for Andrei than reliving his school days—except maybe experiencing a never-ending American prom season, complete with idiotic promposals, plenty of rejection, and zero recourse.

—Satan

THE PEOPLE YOU MEET IN HELL

CHARLES HARRELSON

"THE ONLY REGRET I HAVE IS THAT I'M NOT A MILLIONAIRE."

—CHARLES HARRELSON, CAPITALIST

for Freelancing

Almost everybody is embarrassed by their parents at one point or another, but it could always be worse. Instead of your dad doing a goofy dance in public, he could be popping up in the news for murder like Charles Harrelson, dad of famed actor Woody Harrelson. That's how Woody discovered that his father was a career criminal, con artist, and contract killer who specialized in offing people in power at the behests of other bad dudes—listening to the car radio as a kid in 1973. (Just imagine how awkward Career Day would have been!)

They say if you love what you do, you never work a day in your life, and that was certainly true of the senior Harrelson. (The total lack of conscience and empathy probably helped.) After serving a prison stretch for some lesser crimes, he was released in 1978 and immediately got back to the work he held so dear. It just so happened that, right before drug kingpin Jimmy Chagra was supposed to stand trial in San Antonio in front of US District Judge John H. Wood in 1979, that very judge was shot to death outside of his home. Harrelson ended up back in prison for the hit, but he didn't seem to mind. Notoriety was better than money in his book.

Re: Eternal Damnation

Harrelson likes negative attention, huh? Break out the face paint, because he's our new street performer—a silent, ineffectual mime forced to act out his crimes for unamused passersby.

—Satan

James Urban Ruppert

★★★☆☆
for Ruining Easter

"JAMES RUPPERT REMAINS A CAUTIONARY TALE, A REMINDER THAT EVIL CAN COME IN THE MOST BANAL OF PACKAGES."

— *THE COLUMBUS DISPATCH*, WITH A SICK BURN

If the idea of spending a whole holiday with your family makes you feel like you're going to snap, you're not alone. Even if you do snap and give Uncle Roger a well-earned piece of your mind, you're not alone. But the percentage of people whose gathering-related meltdowns involves murder has got to be pretty small, and James Urban Ruppert is their leader. On Easter Sunday in 1975, he killed all eleven people who had assembled to celebrate: his mother, brother, sister-in-law, and eight nephews and nieces.

James was the typical black sheep, living in his mother's basement in Hamilton, Ohio, while his brother got the girl (James's ex-girlfriend, to be specific), the job, and the family. James's mom set the fuse that Easter by telling her deadbeat drunk of a son to pay up or get out. Then his brother lit it by (*checks notes*) asking him about his car, which James took as an insult. James went back to his room, took out four guns, and started shooting. Then he sat amid the carnage like a weirdo for several hours before finally calling the police and cryptically uttering, "There's been a shooting." James had thought about killing himself but decided that would have been a mortal sin, so he turned himself in instead. So at least he had his priorities straight.

Re: Eternal Damnation

Easter's not my thing, but I can get behind a celebration that involves roasted meat, chocolate bunnies, and hedonistic scavenger hunts. James should be forced to feast forever on stale Peeps for ruining it.

–Satan

RICHARD SPECK

for Nurse Murder

"IT JUST WASN'T
THEIR NIGHT."

—RICHARD SPECK, NIHILISTICALLY

With the exception of Jane Toppan (see page 123), nurses, by and large, are selfless and underpaid, and they put themselves on the line everyday amid all kinds of stress to help their fellow humans (despite a fair few of them not deserving it). And without a speck of humanity, Richard Speck decided to kill a whole bunch of innocent, fresh-faced women still in training for that noble profession. Why? Why not? Speck later said he was high that night, but he also claimed he would have done it sober. So, just your run-of-the-mill mass-murdering monster.

In 1966, Speck broke into a townhouse where nine female nursing students lived and ordered them into a room together so he could bind their hands. Several of the girls naively took his calmness as a good sign rather than as straight-up sociopathy and complied. One by one, he led the young women out of the room to their deaths, strangling and stabbing eight of them. The ninth, Corazon Amurao, hid under a bed until Speck was gone and bravely helped put him behind bars. Thanks to her, it took the jury just forty-nine minutes to find him guilty and sentence him to death. (All things considered, that feels like forty-eight minutes too long.)

Re: Eternal Damnation

Dick will be in Nurse Toppan's care from now on (when she's not busy being tortured herself, that is). But since he can't die again, he'll just *feel* like he's dying for the rest of his afterlife.

—Satan

John Wayne Gacy

★ ★ ★ ★ ★

for Clowning Around

Who would've thought a guy whose side gig was playing "Pogo the Clown" at children's birthday parties would be a monstrous serial killer? Answer: *everybody.* Stephen King even chose a murderous clown for *It* because it was the scariest thing he could think of. But John Wayne Gacy may have been even worse than Pennywise.

Gacy seemed like an ordinary-enough guy, aside from the bizarre choice in hobby. He was married with kids and managing one of his father-in-law's Kentucky Fried Chickens in the 1960s. Apparently, dressing up as a clown was his attempt to seem normal (who's going to tell him?) to cover up the fact that he was secretly raping young men and boys. In 1968, he was sentenced to ten years in prison for sodomy. Jail seemed to suit Gacy for some reason, and he was out in eighteen months for good behavior. He started a construction company, married his second wife, and went right back to being a creep. But this time, he took things further. Over the next several years, he raped and murdered thirty-three men and boys before stashing their bodies in the crawl space of his suburban tract home. He was finally caught in 1978, and it took forensic specialists two years to disentangle and identify the victims' remains. Gacy was executed after fourteen years on death row and a last meal of—wait for it—KFC.

Re: Eternal Damnation

Time for Johnny to find out why people hate clowns, with an endless immersive circus experience and plenty of audience participation.

—Satan

GRISELDA BLANCO

★★★★★
for Shivving the Glass Ceiling

One would think that the person heralded as "The Queen of Cocaine" might have been a Studio 54 regular, or scored a bunch of hits on the disco charts, but those disco divas are just the end users. The real queen of cocaine, Colombian native Griselda Blanco, was the supplier. The queenpin set the whole brutal, deadly, international cocaine trade into motion in the 1970s, first in New York City and then in Miami. (Hey, anything men can do, women can do—including building a drug empire.)

Blanco got started young, kidnapping and killing a ten-year-old when she was just eleven. As a teenager, she married her first of three husbands, all of whom either vastly underestimated their wife or overestimated their own survival skills. Before she dispatched him, husband number two introduced Blanco to her true love: drug trafficking. Blanco's methods were so ruthless, bloody, and wild that her hitmen were known as Cocaine Cowboys, murdering people from their trusty steel steeds (motorcycles). Things were going great—Blanco was making money hand over fist, killing everyone who looked at her sideways, staying one step ahead of the law, and giving future Netflix writers plotlines for days. When she finally did get pinched, she continued to run her operation from the inside. But Blanco may have girl-bossed too close to the sun—after she was released from prison and deported to Colombia, someone used her patented motorcycling-murder method against her in 2012.

Re: Eternal Damnation

Griselda's used to running the show, so let's give her a taste of true powerlessness. She can run the demon daycare center. Talk about the terrible twos!

—Satan

OBTRUSIVE INTERNET AD CREATOR

★ ☆ ☆ ☆ ☆
for Flashing and Distracting

Much like the arbitrary and ever-increasing monthly fees everyone pays big conglomerates to meter out what should be a free and widely available service, having to give up all your personal and private data anytime you want to look at a recipe or check some driving directions is no small price to pay. As part of that breach of the social contract, we get to endure constant ads, shredding our already battered attention spans. They're at the top of the screen, at the bottom of the screen, to the left, to the right, static, rotating—whatever will annoy you enough to get your attention. More recently, that means suffering through a video that pops up right in the middle of the screen and plays automatically until you find the well-hidden, miniscule "X" to get rid of it. And that's if your web browser doesn't crash first. Want to check the weather? Prepare for an absolutely unhinged barrage of flashing ads and pop-ups developed by the bottom-feeders of the tech industry, the bros who couldn't hack it at Apple or Ring. They create the shoddy, hastily designed advertising software that supposedly makes the Internet financially viable in this great American experiment called late-stage capitalism.

Re: Eternal Damnation

Ugh. These guys are the worst. Put them in an escape room of fire- and whip-wielding demons. They can leave when they find the tiny, hidden button that opens the door.

—Satan

RONALD O'BRYAN

for Ruining Halloween

> "I WOULD FORGIVE ALL
> WHO HAVE TAKEN
> PART IN ANY WAY IN
> MY DEATH."
>
> —RONALD O'BRYAN,
> MAGNANIMOUS GUY

Ronald O'Bryan didn't have the body count of, say, most of the other people in this book. In fact, he only committed a single murder. But the nature and impact of that murder are so monumental and maddening that he gets special condemnation. O'Bryan killed his own son for money, an unthinkable crime on its own. But that heinous act would go on to taint Halloween—an innocent night of high-fructose frivolity—for children and parents for generations to come.

In 1974, O'Bryan was deep in debt and couldn't hold down a job. So he concocted a plan as murderous and stupid as any Yosemite Sam ever attempted. First, he took out life insurance policies on his kids that would cover the damage. (Apparently, you *can* put a price on love.) Then he passed out cyanide-laced Pixy Stix to five kids, including Timmy, in the hopes of throwing authorities off his scent when his son turned up dead. Fortunately for the others—and for the police—Timmy was the only one who ate the poisoned treat. The rest were easily traced back to the World's Worst Dad. O'Bryan got what he deserved—death by lethal injection—and millions of parents got a deep mistrust of other people and a new hobby of inspecting candy wrappers for tampering. Thanks, pal!

Re: Eternal Damnation

Ronny gets extra torture for ruining my favorite holiday: a steady diet of the stale, leftover candy corn that gets returned each year to Hell (where it belongs).

—Satan

TED BUNDY

★★★★☆

for Tainted Love

Ted Bundy has always been held up by true-crime fans as some kind of handsome lothario, but it took a minute for this serial killer to find his swagger. He was a smart but awkward kid who had trouble making friends. (His budding psychopathy probably didn't help with that.) As in so many villains' origin stories, Bundy's deadly tendencies hit high gear after he was dumped by his college sweetheart. Instead of crying over rom-coms or hitting the clubs, he became a murderous misogynist, raping and killing as many as one hundred women who looked like the one who got away. (Really putting that psychology degree to work there!)

Women in Bundy's orbit started to disappear around 1974, first in the Pacific Northwest and then in Utah. He avoided suspicion thanks to his post-breakup glow-up and the lack of DNA testing in the 1970s, but he couldn't charm his way out of having a car full of murder paraphernalia during a routine traffic stop. Incredibly, Bundy escaped prison not once but twice after being charged for kidnapping and murder. The second time, he traveled cross-country to Florida— home of all the craziest headlines—and murdered even more women before finally getting the chair in 1989. But thanks to portrayals by dashing actors like Mark Harmon and Zac Efron, people have oddly conflicting feels about the lunatic.

Re: Eternal Damnation

It's a shame Ted died before dating apps existed. He deserves to experience all the fun of being ghosted, rejected, and stalked. And he will, on Hell's premier service: Arson.

—Satan

THE PEOPLE YOU MEET IN HELL

DENNIS NILSEN

for Plumbing the Depths

Dennis Nilsen was a real DIY kind of guy, for better and for worse. Mostly worse. When he used tools and worked with his hands, it wasn't to renovate the bathroom in his London flat—it was to kill people and desecrate their bodies. (Although, installing a garbage disposal might have kept him out of prison a little while longer.)

Between 1978 and 1983, Nilsen killed as many as fifteen guys he'd lured home from local bars. His hands-on murder method of choice: strangulation—an act that takes way more time and work than the movies would have you believe. It's an awful way to make people spend their last minutes on Earth, but it wasn't his worst crime. After his victims were dead, he'd dissect them like that creepy kid in biology class who was always a little too eager to slice and dice frogs. When he was done experimenting, he'd burn the remains and shove what was left down his drain. Like any rule-breaking city dweller, Nilsen was done in by complaining neighbors. The other residents of his building started reporting clogged drains. Even Nilsen himself called, apparently not putting two and two together. Plumbers quickly traced the blockages (mostly bones) to his top-floor flat.

Re: Eternal Damnation

Dennis gets off on death? He can tend to my wife's gardens. And if he so much as underwaters a succulent, he can take a spin through Hell's sewage system.

–Satan

ROBERT WILLIAM PICKTON

for Giving Pigs a Bad Name

> "I WAS JUST DOING WHAT I WAS TOLD TO DO BY THE VOICES IN MY HEAD."
>
> —ROBERT WILLIAM PICKTON, SANELY

Pigs are adorable, fun, intelligent creatures who've gotten a bad rap. Notorious pig farmer/human butcher Robert William "Willy" Pickton doesn't deserve to be classified among them. For one thing, pigs would bathe if they could. Pickton, not so much, and it didn't help that his mother sent him and his brother to school in mud-caked, manure-soaked clothes. The fact that it took authorities years to figure out that this repugnant excuse for a man was hacking up humans alongside his livestock is frankly absurd. No one has ever looked the part more than this guy. But, then again, they weren't too concerned with the kinds of humans he was butchering.

Pickton started soliciting drug-addicted prostitutes back to his farm as early as 1979, then crudely and callously butchering them and feeding them to his starving pigs. He wasn't arrested until 2002, when police finally searched his sprawling farm and found items belonging to the missing women . . . like their skulls and bones. That's when they realized Pickton was probably feeding his victims' remains to the pigs (and to the unlucky humans who bought his "pork" products). He was charged with twenty-six murders, but an undercover cop posing as a criminal got a confession of even more along with Pickton's statement of remorse—not for killing forty-nine women, of course, but rather that he didn't make it to a nice, even fifty. Pickton chalked it up to getting "sloppy" toward the end of his years-long murder habit.

Re: Eternal Damnation

We're going to make sure Willy is squeaky clean at all times, with round-the-clock showers and lots of cruelty-free soap.

—Satan

LONNIE DAVID FRANKLIN JR.

for Sleeplessness

Lonnie David Franklin Jr. didn't earn his horror-movie-character-esque nickname, "The Grim Sleeper," because he killed in his sleep or killed others while they slept. Authorities dubbed him that because they thought a compulsive serial killer took a restful fourteen-year break in the middle of a murderous crime spree spanning decades. Odds are pretty good that he didn't, though. Franklin had *hundreds* of trophy photos in his home when he was arrested, including those of the ten known victims. Plus, he was a retired garbage man who knew more than a few ways to dispose of a body. But sure, LAPD, he just stopped for fourteen years.

Despite a prison stay and a dishonorable discharge from the Army for sexually assaulting a teenager in Germany, Franklin was described by neighbors as a friendly guy. Little did they know he was offing Black prostitutes in his spare time. After literal decades of striking out, authorities caught the breaks they desperately needed: DNA evidence linking a 2010 murder to several others from the early 1980s and 2000s and a familial match in Franklin's son Christopher, who had given a sample on his way into prison in 2009. (Heck of a family tree!) Now that they knew their killer, they just needed a little confirmatory DNA. And they got it—from a discarded pizza crust picked up by a cop in busboy's clothing. Talk about watching your carbs.

Re: Eternal Damnation

Lonnie definitely wasn't sleeping through those fourteen years, but there's no rest for the wicked down here. Every time he nods off—BANG—a gong rings out.

—Satan

"FREE BIRD" GUY

★★☆☆☆

for Originality

If a joke is funny once, then it's funny a zillion more times, right? Isn't that the rule of comedy? No, it's not. And the guy who shouts "Free Bird" at a concert because he thought it was funny that one time he heard somebody say what was already a cringy cliché deserves a spot on this list. Asking a band who isn't Lynyrd Skynyrd to play "Free Bird" isn't fun. It isn't clever. It's just heckling a band who's trying to get through a show you probably paid to attend, which makes it both tedious and offensive. In short: it makes you sound like an idiot. Bands have gotten so tired of these people that they'll often throw the dad-joker out. But, occasionally, something worse happens—the band will punish the entire audience by playing all nine long minutes of the song (whether or not they have the chops to do it). No one wants that. You don't even want that. You just want the attention for a lame joke that isn't even yours. Don't be that guy. And if you are that guy, you'll pay for it in the afterlife.

Re: Eternal Damnation

If they think it's so great, they can listen to that song—and only that song—for the rest of their afterlife. But in a soundproof room, so I don't have to hear it.

—Satan

WILLIAM UNEK

★★★★☆
for Checking All the Boxes

Talk about a triple threat. William Unek is the rare individual that criminologists would classify as a mass murderer *and* a serial killer *and* a spree killer. Even more impressive—he used an axe instead of the typical and much easier automatic weapon to mow down his many victims in one go. Something snapped in the police constable in 1954, and he killed twenty-one people in the Belgian Congo within an hour and a half before escaping to a British territory.

Unbelievably, Unek continued his life as a free man and police officer there for another three years. But once an unstable psychopath, always an unstable psychopath. In 1957, he got into a disagreement with his boss and went on another tear. The first killing spree must have been too taxing, though, because he added a rifle, a knife, and fire to his second one, killing thirty-six men, women, and children. And he did it all in a police uniform. The only murder Unek bothered to cover up was that of his wife—he set their shared hut on fire for good measure. This time, it only took nine days for authorities to catch up with him. Sure, they burned down a Good Samaritan's house in the process of smoking Unek out. And, yes, Unek died from the burns. But they got their man!

Re: Eternal Damnation

```
Willy has quite the temper. He's going to need to keep
a lid on that as a member of Hell's customer service
department. And if he can't, he can take a time-out in
that burning hut of his.
```

—Satan

THE PEOPLE YOU MEET IN HELL

Harrison "Marty" Graham

★☆☆☆☆

for Lame Excuses

Plenty of killers blame other people for their crimes, but not many confess to the crimes of other people. Serial killer Harrison "Marty" Graham was unique in that way . . . and a few others. For one thing, Marty wasn't his nickname; it was one of his four personalities—the good one. Technically, "Frank" was the murderous misogynist stacking dead bodies in his apartment like Jenga blocks. But it's pretty hard to punish just one of a person's identities.

When Graham was evicted from his Philadelphia apartment in 1987 for the increasingly foul odor emanating from it, authorities knew what they were in for. (The question is, how did his neighbors *not*?) They found the deeply decomposed bodies of seven women strewn about the place—on the bed, under piles of garbage, and stuffed in between mattresses. When brought in for questioning, Graham said that the bodies had been there when he moved in, and he'd just dealt with them. As you do. And when that didn't fly for some strange reason, he fessed up for "Frank." A judge sentenced all four personalities to life in prison—even "Junior," the two-year-old whose best friend was a Cookie Monster doll he slept with, talked to, and took with him everywhere. (So. Many. Red. Flags.)

Re: Eternal Damnation

```
The judicial system may not be able to separate
personalities, but we can. "Frank" will face eternity
on his own, cleaning up after the smelliest torture
methods until everything smells lemony fresh.
```

–Satan

Jeffrey Dahmer

★★★★★
for an Unhealthy Appetite

Into a society already jaded and unmoved by tales of serial killers came Jeffrey Dahmer, a guy so deranged he makes your worst online-dating stories sound like rom-coms. Dahmer didn't just kill his hookups (and then hook up with his kills)—he trapped and tortured them, chopped them up like rump roasts, cooked them, and ate whatever edible remains remained. Dahmer had the flavors that made Milwaukee famous! Thankfully, his days in the kitchen from Hell were numbered.

In July of 1991, Dahmer picked up Tracy Edwards in a Cream City bar and took him home for a nude modeling session. (Sounds legit.) There, he drugged, tortured, and handcuffed the man. But Edwards managed to escape, find two cops, and lead them back to Dahmer's apartment, where they were met with a stench that would make Oscar the Grouch blanch. Turns out, the freshly severed head in the fridge was a dead giveaway.

Dahmer was convicted of committing seventeen murders over more than a decade. Once in prison, he begged to be moved from solitary confinement into the general population. But another inmate killed him for being creepy. Be careful what you wish for, folks!

Re: Eternal Damnation

The "Butcher of Milwaukee" gets the best that nature and food scientists have to offer! Soy milk, aquafaba, tofu, veggie patties—his avocado-colored fridge will be bursting at the seams with vegan food. Let's see if we can't bring down his cholesterol while he's here.

—Satan

Yang Xinhai

★★★★☆
for Improvisation

"WHEN I KILLED PEOPLE, I HAD A DESIRE [TO KILL MORE]. THIS INSPIRED ME TO KILL MORE."

—YANG XINHAI, SIMPLE GUY

Some geniuses invent games for the masses; Yang Xinhai decided to put his considerable brain power toward playing a real-life version of Clue instead, with him as the killer. Between 1999 and 2003, the Chinese serial killer dubbed "The Monster Killer" by the media (it's not remotely clever, but, hey, it's accurate) left a trail of sixty-seven bodies behind him before being caught and executed for his crimes. And anyone with that kind of body count is bound to get bored and start branching out, right?

Hell hath no fury like a psychopath scorned. In a tale that's all too familiar, Yang channeled his rage at being rejected by an ex-girlfriend (because she found out about his prior convictions for theft and attempted rape—who can blame her?) into numerous violent crimes. From the age of seventeen, his transgressions escalated from theft to attempted rape to repeated rapes and murders. When he was thirty-two, he decided to have a little fun with his killing sprees and try his hand at improv. He'd pick a house, then kill everyone inside with whatever he found on hand, including shovels, axes, and cleavers. (Apparently, no candlesticks or wrenches were available.) He'd also assault his female victims if the mood struck him. Yang entered the homes of sleeping families and butchered its occupants like a horror-movie maniac with a grudge thirteen times. The jury was just as unforgiving, sentencing him to a bullet in under an hour.

Re: Eternal Damnation

Xinhai can go through his afterlife never having what he needs when he needs it, whether it's a door to protect him from an axe-wielding demon or toilet paper in a bathroom stall.

—Satan

THE PEOPLE YOU MEET IN HELL

Public Clipper

★☆☆☆☆
for Nailing Annoyance

Not to body-shame here, but the human body is absolutely disgusting. It's a bag of wet meat through which electricity runs, and there's a scary skeleton inside it all. For however long as it lasts, it requires constant maintenance, like brushing teeth, removing wax from ears, and trimming nails. Almost exclusively, all of those things are done in the privacy of one's own home—and usually in one's bathroom at that—away from polite society and prying and impressionable eyes. Why? Because it will ruin your day to see another person groom themselves like a monkey in a zoo enclosure. (Even when monkeys do it, it's not cute.) But for some unfathomable reason, a handful of people—the crudest, most unaware of the bunch—seem to think it's acceptable to trim their nails not just in public, but in close quarters with others. This may be one of the grossest facets of human maintenance that there is. No one wants to hear the sound of things getting snipped off the human body while hurtling through the sky or underground tunnels in a tin can they can't escape from. And then there are those especially craven few who hold and trim their bare and who-knows-how-clean feet in the presence of others before tucking into a homemade sandwich (*shudder*). To all the public clippers, hand and foot alike: we can see you, and we hate you.

Re: Eternal Damnation

Like a boggart from *Harry Potter*, whatever annoys these folks most will appear when they're at their most vulnerable. It's only fair.

—Satan

RICH AND FAMOUS AND AWFUL

CHAPTER 5

Thomas Dartmouth "Daddy" Rice

for Profiting Off Racism

Some unemployed actors put on one-man plays to try to get their name out there. Others do bits on YouTube. But only the most abhorrent ones resort to racist theatrics to stay in the spotlight. Who would do such a thing? A few members of Congress come to mind, along with mid-1800s minstrel performer and unimpressive white guy Thomas Dartmouth "Daddy" Rice. Rice donned blackface, adopted the moniker Jim Crow, and acted out highly exaggerated and insulting stereotypes about enslaved people using song and dance, to the absolute delight of white audiences.

Today, Rice is considered the father of minstrelsy—a type of theater that's unique to America, for pretty obvious reasons—which makes him wholly responsible for perpetuating the falsehood that Black people were lazy, stupid, and less than human. And the crowds loved him for it. Suddenly, the struggling actor was the talk of towns across the country. The name Jim Crow, which he appropriated from a Black performer (no surprise there), took on a life of its own as a racial slur for the next fifty years. But the horrifying ripple effects don't stop there! Anyone who's taken an eighth-grade civics class knows that the name also became synonymous with the "whites only" laws of the post-Reconstruction era. Quite the legacy!

Re: Eternal Damnation

He just wanted to be a real actor? Cool. It's an afterlife of performing in poorly attended off-, off-Broadway plays for this guy, complete with scorching-hot spotlights and cheap ramen for every meal.

—Satan

ALEXANDER GRAHAM BELL

★★☆☆☆
for Patent Thievery

"BEFORE ANYTHING
ELSE, PREPARATION IS THE
KEY TO SUCCESS."

—ALEXANDER GRAHAM BELL,
PREPARING TO STEAL IDEAS

The telephone—the incredible invention that instantly connects people in real time across thousands of miles (and the thing that you now keep on silent and refuse to use as a telephone) is credited as a historic and heroic creation of Alexander Graham Bell. Only one problem: he pretty much stole the idea from rival inventor Elisha Gray. So the story goes, Gray was working on a similar invention at the same time when Bell paid off patent examiner Zenas Fisk Wilber, an old army buddy of his lawyer, to tip him off should Gray file a patent. Apparently, Wilber had bills (read: gambling debts) to pay, so he took the deal and gave Bell a sneak peek at Gray's patent diagrams.

Bell used Gray's liquid transmitter design to build his own phone, patent it, and keep all the credit and money for himself. He made the first successful telephone call on March 10, 1876, uttering the famous words, "Mr. Watson, come here, I want to see you." But what he really meant was, "Mr. Watson, come here, I want to gloat over my stolen invention." And then he proceeded to sue anyone who tried to challenge his patent—including Gray, who had some pretty convincing evidence of the theft. But history is written by the victors, and the wealthy and influential Bell clearly won that round.

Re: Eternal Damnation

Bell wants the credit? Great, he can deal with the fallout—namely, all the telemarketers. He'll suffer an unending barrage of calls that won't stop ringing until he answers and engages.

–Satan

THOMAS EDISON

★★★★☆
for Business Acumen

"IF YOU WANT TO SUCCEED, GET SOME ENEMIES."

—THOMAS EDISON,
FAN OF FRIENDLY COMPETITION

As they say, history is written by the victors (see Alexander Graham Bell on page 165—the one you read two seconds ago), which is why Thomas Edison has been able to convince generations that he was some great inventor. After all, he held 1,093 patents. But, like Mr. Bell, Edison wasn't necessarily the rightful owner of all of them. He was a better businessman than he was an inventor, and a viciously cutthroat one at that.

Like the wealthy, influential, and entitled guy-about-town that he was, Edison was known to steal inventions and patent them in his own name without a shred of guilt. When competitors got too close, he'd destroy their stuff and hog all the glory, royalties, and money for himself. He even tried to create a monopoly over the film industry by claiming to have invented the motion-picture camera and suing anyone who used it. He also electrocuted a number of innocent animals at the urging of the Society for the Prevention of Cruelty to Animals (bizarrely enough) to help them humanely kill an ornery elephant in 1903. But Edison didn't stop there—he decided to use electrical euthanasia to bolster his film career (by filming it, like a monster) *and* stick it to George Westinghouse, whom he was battling over whose electricity was better. Think about that the next time you flip on a light switch!

Re: Eternal Damnation

The spotlight stealer can soak it up down here . . . as a circus clown in slapstick bits where elephants make him look stupid. Justice for Topsy!

—Satan

KENESAW MOUNTAIN LANDIS

★★★★☆
for Impeding Progress

As a federal judge, Kenesaw Mountain Landis was known for no-nonsense judgments against big business, except when that business was baseball. In those cases, he was "restoring the sport's integrity." (Because getting rich to play a game has the ring of fairness to it.) Landis's glaring bias worked out pretty well for him; he increased his salary almost seven fold with a career change from judge to baseball commissioner. And the sport suited him. It was clear-cut, all-American, and as lily-white and boring as a bowl of plain yogurt—just how he liked it.

It's no secret that Major League Baseball was officially, structurally, and systemically racist for much of the early twentieth century, and Landis made sure of it. Integrity might have been his claim to baseball fame, but integration would happen over his dead body. (Which it did.) Jackie Robinson broke the color line in 1947—a solid three years after Landis died. And there were plenty of other players of color who were as good as, if not better than, Robinson but never got the chance to play in the majors. With Landis dead, the MLB was able to wiggle out from under his oppressively white thumb. But it would take another *seventy-five years* to get his racist mug off the MVP plaques handed to players of all races. Progress!

Re: Eternal Damnation

Kenny seems like he could use a little perspective. Maybe spending his afterlife on Disney's "It's a Small World" ride will help straighten him out.

—Satan

STAGE PARENT

★★☆☆☆
for Not Kidding Around

Stage parents are like mosquitoes: they buzz around, suck the life out of you, and leave you with an itch that won't go away. Countless horror stories about child actors don't deter these people from attempting to inflict the same fate on their own kid. No, no, their kid is going to be a STAR. Instead of protecting their little one, they'll shove them face first into the Hollywood machine, which is both symbolically predatory and filled with literal predators. But, hey, they'll get to live their sad, broken dreams vicariously through their progeny without having to do any of the work or be exploited themselves or give up their own childhood. Maybe they'll even fulfill the other part of the cliché: stealing their kid's hard-earned money. And if things don't work out (because— let's face it—there are a lot more Dana Platos than Jason Batemans), they'll add their bitter disappointment on top of all that childhood trauma. Good parenting! No notes.

Re: Eternal Damnation

Stage parents will be forced to sit through endless community theater productions of *Annie* from the front row, with an amateur videographer constantly smacking them in the head with their giant video camera.

—**Satan**

David O. Selznick

★★★★★
for Toxic Bossing

> "THERE MIGHT HAVE BEEN GOOD MOVIES
> IF THERE HAD BEEN NO MOVIE INDUSTRY."
> —DAVID O. SELZNICK, THE PROBLEM

Hollywood has changed a lot since the golden age of filmmaking, when actors were held to stifling contracts, worked twenty-hour days, and suffered the whims of predatory and power-mad bosses like David O. Selznick. Oh, wait, no it hasn't. And Selznick himself has a lot to do with that. He set the bar (on the ground) for abusive producers and got the ball rolling on the bad side of the #MeToo movement.

Selznick made big moves to create an illustrious career that included hits like *A Star Is Born* in 1937 and *Gone with the Wind* in 1939. But his egomaniacal behavior turned straight-up maniacal with amphetamine-fueled meddling and nonsensical, sixty-page, middle-of-the-night memos. Plus, he was a menace to the women on the set. Shirley Temple wrote in her memoir that she'd been warned to avoid him when he was in stocking feet—apparently a telltale sign that he was on the prowl. (Hey, everyone's got their thing.) When he cornered the seventeen-year-old in his office behind a mechanically locked door, and she saw the socks, she knew she was in trouble. But the "amorous but overweight producer" was no match for the agility of America's sweetheart. Who knows how many actresses and secretaries weren't as nimble (or as ready to spill the tea)? But, hey, that's Hollywood, baby!

Re: Eternal Damnation

Let's dress Dave up like a young Miss Temple so he can perform her "Good Ship Lollipop" routine on demand in front of Hell's song-and-dance-loving demons. What they do with him behind locked doors is their business.

–Satan

THE PEOPLE YOU MEET IN HELL

COLONEL TOM PARKER

"I'M NOT IN SHOW BUSINESS, I'M IN THE MONEY MAKING BUSINESS."

—COLONEL TOM PARKER, ACCURATELY

for Getting Away with It

Colonel Tom Parker is best known for two things: being grossly overweight and managing one of the greatest musicians of all time, Elvis Presley. Parker knew what he'd found in the hip-shaking singer, which is why he signed him to a criminally large 50-percent management fee and whored the boy out all over Hollywood. Presley would generate $1 billion in his lifetime, but when he died in 1977, he had a net worth of $4.9 million. Where'd the rest go? Mostly to Parker.

But here's where things get really interesting. (No offense to the King.) Colonel Tom Parker was actually Dutch native Andreas van Kuijk, a carney and a conman who came to America in 1929. He did enlist in the US Army, but he got discharged as a private for *being a literal psychopath*. Hint: That last part's important. Although "Parker" was milking his cash cow dry, he refused to do lucrative European tours, ostensibly due to his little immigration issue. But that would have been easy enough for him to fix. You know what's harder to clear up? Murder. Kuijk coincidentally disappeared from Holland without warning or money right around the time a local grocer's wife was found beaten to death. Her killer remains a mystery, but, for what it's worth, everyone who'd ever met Kuijk assumed he was guilty. Still, he died fat, happy, and rich at the ripe old age of eighty-seven. The American dream!

Re: Eternal Damnation

This calls for a movie marathon! Andreas can watch every terrible movie he made Elvis do—plus that Baz Luhrmann abomination—on an endless loop.

—Satan

SPADE COOLEY

★★★★☆
for Being a Country Song

"TODAY IS THE FIRST DAY OF THE REST OF MY LIFE."

—SPADE COOLEY, SECONDS BEFORE DROPPING DEAD

Donnell Clyde "Spade" Cooley was a country-music superstar in the early 1950s, back when you could look and sound like Barney Fife with a fiddle and be considered cool. The "king of Western swing," as he liked to call himself (because anyone who knew anything about music had already bestowed this moniker on bandleader Bob Wills) appeared in fifty movies, played to crowds around the country, and got a star on the Hollywood Walk of Fame. He was so beloved that the jurors in his murder trial even cried and hugged him after convicting him for killing his wife with his bare hands. Awesome guy.

Cooley spent hours beating and torturing Ella Mae Evans in April 1961 for the murder-worthy crime of having affairs with homosexual men. (Yeah, that could have been projection from Cooley, who worried he might be gay and so had countless affairs with women who were not his wife.) The couple's teenage daughter witnessed the whole thing and helped put her dad behind bars. But don't worry—he didn't actually do hard time. Cooley had plenty of fans inside and out, some of whom got him a spot at a more relaxed prison, the promise of parole after only a few years, and a three-day furlough to play a concert (after which he dropped dead from heart failure—even karma gave the guy a wide berth).

Re: Eternal Damnation

We love a self-loathing king down here. Let's give Donny a chance to confront his own demons by playing the gay-bar circuit.

–Satan

THE PEOPLE YOU MEET IN HELL

JIMMY SAVILE

★★★★☆
for Hiding in Plain Sight

There are few instances in history where America comes off better than other countries in the press, but the posthumous scandal of Jimmy Savile is one of them. Dick Clark used his power and influence as the host of *American Bandstand* to create a wholesome media empire (and make a lot of money). As host of the British equivalent, *Top of the Pops*, beginning in 1964, Jimmy Savile used his celebrity and power to become one of his country's most prolific sex offenders.

Despite looking like the Crypt Keeper with a Prince Valiant haircut, Savile sweet-talked his way into the lives, homes, and pants of British citizens over the course of fifty years in the public eye. Even Margaret Thatcher and now-King Charles were fans. But in 2012, a year after he died, more than 400 credible victims—young, old, and even dead—were discovered. Yep, in addition to being a predator, he was also a necrophiliac (which makes him sitting with his mother's dead body for five days even more disturbing). Most heinous of all is that he used charitable visits to children's homes, schools, and hospitals around the country as "hunting" trips. The man even joked about hoping that his good deeds would balance out his depravity on live television, and they knighted him! Quite a bar the British set there.

Re: Eternal Damnation

It makes total sense that this was the man who helped King Charles commune with the commoners. He can put those PR talents to good use as the hype man for every despicable soul who enters Hell. How's that for penance, Jimmy?

—**Satan**

MORRIS LEVY

for Killer Business Instincts

"YOU WANT ROYALTIES?
THEN GO TO ENGLAND!"

—MORRIS LEVY, CRIMINALLY

The American music industry circa the mid-twentieth century was not for the faint of heart. (See Colonel Tom Parker on page 171.) And Morris Levy fit right in. One of the most awful and all-too-pervasive practices in the business—using shady tactics to make millions off underpaid artists—just so happened to be a specialty of his. They didn't call him "the octopus" and "the godfather of the music industry" because of his curious, warm, and paternal demeanor. The man was mobbed up, specifically with the Genovese crime family, and had an arm in every aspect of the business. He was such a caricature of Mafioso culture that they even based a Sopranos character on him. (That's how you know you've made it in New Jersey.)

Levy manipulated deals to fall in his favor and, when people fought back, he used his cement-shoe-lacing reputation to intimidate them into shutting up. Over the course of his decades-long career in the industry, Levy treated royalties like a personal affront—except when it came to his own, of course. That's why he credited himself as a contributing songwriter on hit records. The "accomplished lyricist" was finally pinched by the Feds in 1986, but he didn't spend a day in prison—mostly because he died of cancer. The man always had an out.

Re: Eternal Damnation

I'm all for organized crime, but those oldies compilations Moishe helped create in order to skirt copyright law and pocket the cash are torture. Specifically, his. He can listen to them on an endless loop.

–Satan

THE PEOPLE YOU MEET IN HELL

THE DEVIL'S ADVOCATE

★ ★ ★ ★ ☆
for Expert-Level Irritation

It's right there in the name—these constantly contradictory nightmare humans were put on Earth to torture anyone trying to have a pleasant conversation. You'll be talking with friends about the merits of dogs and cats, and this person will jump in and argue that parakeets are the superior pet. Or you're discussing your favorite beach read, and suddenly they're insisting that Russian literature is the only thing worth reading. It's like they get some sort of sick kick out of making everything harder than it needs to be or think their controversial opinions make them more interesting. Newsflash, buddy: You're not edgy, you're annoying. And you probably don't even believe your own BS. So next time you feel the urge to be contrarian just for the sake of it, resist. Try being agreeable for once. Who knows, you might even make a new friend or two! But if you feel the need to keep being argumentative for argument's sake, be warned: it's not going to end well for you.

Re: Eternal Damnation

Nothing knocks the bluster out of these windbags like winning their make-believe argument. Let's surround every devil's advocate with yes-men who agree with everything they say. That'll shut them up.

—Satan

RICH AND FAMOUS AND AWFUL

IKE TURNER

for Toxic Masculinity

"I HAVE NO REGRETS IN MY LIFE."

—IKE TURNER, MAN OF CONVICTION(S)

A lot of successful musicians make bad choices. Like, *a lot*. But those choices usually end up being funny or teachable footnotes in the straight-to-streaming movies about their careers (with a few glaring exceptions; see John Phillips, page 180). So imagine how terrible Ike Turner must have been—or how terrible a musician he was—for his drug-fueled abuse of his superstar wife to be the only thing anyone remembers about him.

In 1951, Turner and his Kings of Rhythm recorded "Rocket 88," a song regarded by many music historians as the first rock-and-roll song. But Turner didn't get a taste of real success until he paired up with Anna Mae Bullock—aka Tina Turner. You'd think he'd be grateful to his golden goose, but no. He chose the road most traveled by insecure men: cheating, taking drugs, and nearly killing his wife via brutal beatings.

Tina finally dropped the dead weight in 1976 and rose to superstardom. Ike, on the other hand, spent eighteen months in the pen for cocaine possession, missing his own induction into the Rock and Roll Hall of Fame. He overdosed nineteen whole years later at the age of seventy-six, having not learned a single lesson in his lifetime. (Although it was less the fact that he *did* coke and more the fact that he *did coke at the age of seventy-six* that killed him.)

Re: Eternal Damnation

Ike can play Tina in our nightly drag shows, with one little adjustment: every strum electrocutes him and triggers a giant hand to slap him across the face.

—Satan

THE PEOPLE YOU MEET IN HELL

JERRY LEE LEWIS

"IF I'M GOING TO HELL, I'M GOING THERE PLAYING THE PIANO."

—JERRY LEE LEWIS, ACCURATELY

for All the Things

The rock and roll music of the 1950s might be pretty tame in comparison to that of later decades, but, back then, it was a rebellious, inflammatory sound that squares worried would corrupt their screaming teenagers. And with good reason: music might evolve over time, but musicians rarely do—especially when they're surrounded by alcohol and attractive groupies. Jerry Lee Lewis was one of those worrisome rock stars seemingly possessed by their own music and ego while rocking it out on the piano for "Great Balls of Fire" and the presciently titled "High School Confidential." But being a hell-raiser doesn't actually earn you a place in Hell. For that, you need to throw a little incest, assault, statutory rape, bigamy, adultery, or murder into the mix. And Lewis had all of the above on his playlist.

From trying to strangle a teacher to shooting his bass player and abusing each of his seven wives, Lewis's life was chock-full of bad behavior. But he's most notorious for marrying his thirteen-year-old cousin, Myra Gale Brown, in 1957, when he was twenty-two—while still married to wives number one and two. (Perhaps unsurprisingly, cousins marrying each other was not a rare occurrence in the Lewis family.) All three fared better than wife number five, who died under mysterious and most likely Lewis-related circumstances. Incredibly, Lewis died of old age—and from the many, many drugs he took—in 2022.

> **Re: Eternal Damnation**
>
> There'll be no more shakin' for Jerry. The talented pianist can play quiet ballads in the common room of Hell's retirement home.
>
> **—Satan**

JOHN PHILLIPS

★★★★★
for Ick Factor

"THE ROAD TO STARDOM IS USUALLY A PRETTY SLEAZY ONE, AS FAR AS I'M CONCERNED."

— JOHN PHILLIPS, AUTOBIOGRAPHICALLY

John Phillips was the very essence of the 1960s—all gentle harmonies, hard drugs, and free love—and he went all in on the last two. This guy was so wild and strung out on acid, heroin, and anything else he could get his nose on that *Keith Richards* once kicked him out of a party. Talk about a come-to-Jesus moment. But addiction was just one of the songwriter's sins, and far from the worst one.

Phillips had the kind of complicated (read: terrible) relationship with women you'd expect from a superstar in the '60s. He left his first wife for seventeen-year-old Michelle Gilliam, marrying her and forming the Mamas and the Papas soon after. And she wasn't the last teenager he set his sights on. According to his daughter Mackenzie Phillips, she and her dear old dad had a drug-fueled, decade-long sexual relationship that started in 1979, when she was nineteen—on the eve of her wedding to Jeff Sessler, in case the incest wasn't creepy enough on its own. Some claimed John would never, but this was a guy who took his then-five-year-old daughter to the Virgin Islands with a bunch of musicians and a quart of LSD. He definitely wasn't winning any Father of the Year awards. But, hey, such great harmonies.

Re: Eternal Damnation

This man needs Jesus. And he'll get to hear about Him all day, every day, when he answers the door to the only visitors he's allowed in his sober living home: a pair of overzealous Jehovah's Witnesses.

—Satan

THE PEOPLE YOU MEET IN HELL

LITTERBUG

★☆☆☆☆
for Trashy Behavior

Ah, litterbugs. The unsung heroes of laziness and disregard for the environment. They toss their trash out the car window like it's confetti on New Year's Eve, and they couldn't care less about the consequences. The world is their garbage can, and we're all just living in it.

What's the deal with these people? Did they miss the part of kindergarten where we learned to clean up after ourselves? Did they never see that PSA with the crying Native American dude? Or are they just so self-absorbed that they think their empty soda can is someone else's problem? Honestly, it's just sad. They're missing out on the joy of picking up their own trash, feeling the satisfaction of doing the right thing, and maybe even impressing a potential date with their responsible nature. Plus, think of all the cool litter-picker-upper tools they could buy! So, to all you litterbugs out there: shape up, pick up, and let's keep this world a little cleaner, one crumpled-up napkin at a time. Or else.

Re: Eternal Damnation

These human garbage heaps are hereby sentenced to an eternity of being followed around by irritable seagulls. No matter where they go or what they do, the seagulls are always there, squawking obnoxiously and pecking at them for scraps.

—Satan

BERNARD MADOFF

for $cheming

"THE WHOLE
GOVERNMENT IS A
PONZI SCHEME."

—BERNIE MADOFF,
MASTER OF DEFLECTION

When it comes to all the Ponzi schemers in history, you have to ask yourself: what exactly was the endgame there? They knew they didn't actually have the money, and that someone would come knocking for it at some point. It was always going to end in jail. Really, they're just lucky that people don't use pitchforks anymore. But Bernie Madoff seemed completely stumped by his arrest for having *made off* (yep, deal with it) with millions of other people's money.

Madoff was the financial whiz who created the NASDAQ stock exchange and advised the Securities and Exchange Commission (delightfully ironic). But did he continue to use his powers for good? Of course not. Instead, he headed up a financial-services firm that attracted superrich and famous clients with the (completely fabricated) promise of consistently high returns—a classic Ponzi scheme using some investors' money to pay off others and praying the whole thing didn't crumble. But, of course, it did crumble. Analyst Harry Markopolos uncovered massive fraud and brought the SEC and financial press a-knockin' in 2008. But the money was long gone—Madoff's $65 billion portfolio was now worth a scant $100 million. He got 150 years in prison for chicanery of the highest order, and the public got to sympathize with the ultrarich people he swindled. What a win-win!

Re: Eternal Damnation

Bernie can spend eternity playing and losing the longest and most annoying board game in history—Monopoly. Let's see you try your scheming when you land on a hoteled-up Park Place for the 600th time!

–Satan

PHIL SPECTOR

for Deadly Eccentricity

> "...THE DEVIL WON'T LET ME INTO HELL BECAUSE HE'S AFRAID THAT I'LL TAKE OVER."
>
> —PHIL SPECTOR, HILARIOUSLY

There's eccentric, and then there's crazy, and there's a fine line between the two. Music producer Phil Spector did a jig on that line for decades before finally and irredeemably crossing it. And man, did he go out in style—turning up to his trial for the 2003 murder of Lana Clarkson in ostentatious limousines, wearing elaborate outfits with wigs and high heels, and sporting a brand-new twenty-six-year-old bride. Somehow, it didn't help his case. He got nineteen years to life. The fact that his chauffeur was an eyewitness who saw Spector come out of his house with bloody hands and a gun saying, "I think I killed someone" probably didn't help either. Nor did Spector's long history of waving guns at people.

Spector was considered a genius in the music world. He created the "Wall of Sound," that impenetrable, echo-loaded force of magical music that defined 1960s girl groups. He was also an absolute nut. The man regularly had gun-waving fits at recording artists—*his paying clients*. He also tormented women, including his wife and lead singer of the Ronettes, Ronnie Spector. After divorcing him in 1974, she said he'd kept her prisoner in their home and threatened to kill her and put her in a gold coffin he kept in the basement. And five separate women testified at his trial that he'd held them at gunpoint. So, clearly, Clarkson's death was completely unexpected. No red flags to see here!

Re: Eternal Damnation

We see Phil's "Wall of Sound" and raise him an entire room of sound, blasting his own cacophonous music until it drives him sane.

–Satan

THE PEOPLE YOU MEET IN HELL

JAMES LEVINE

★★★☆☆
for **Classically Predatory Behavior**

"AS A CONDUCTOR,
MY JOB IS TO BRING OUT THE
BEST IN THE MUSICIANS
AND THE MUSIC."

—JAMES LEVINE,
WHILE LYING DOWN ON THE JOB

Acclaimed conductor (and man who resembles a lumpy potato wearing a small poodle on its head) James Levine spent more than forty years shaping the sound of New York City's prestigious Metropolitan Opera. He led more than 2,500 performances, won ten Grammys, and brought in one of the biggest salaries in the business. And like a lot of old white guys at the top of their game, he brought his whole illustrious career crashing down on his own head by being a predatory creep.

Let's just say that Levine had a *hands-on approach* when it came to working with young musicians—particularly men in their teens and early twenties. After several came forward in 2017 to accuse Levine of assault, coercion, grooming, and retaliation for refusal, the Met dropped him like a hot potato covered in esophagus-searing ghost-pepper sauce. (It's almost like they knew the accusations were true without even having to investigate.) Levine tried to sue for defamation, but the Met had the receipts, so he left his profession in disgrace instead. He did not, however, face charges for being a monster thanks to some predator-friendly laws at the time of the abuse, back in the 1980s. Yay, justice!

Re: Eternal Damnation

Jimmy will be forced to listen to parodies of classical works, like that old answering machine tape set to Beethoven's Fifth Symphony that goes, "Nobody's home/nobody's hoooooome," until his ears bleed.

–Satan

THE PEOPLE YOU MEET IN HELL

EUGENE LANDY

for the Hustle

What kind of monster exploits a sensitive artistic genius and obviously mentally ill victim of abuse for his own personal financial gain? Eugene Landy, one of the most depraved people to ever work in the entertainment industry not named Weinstein. In the 1970s, when Beach Boys mastermind Brian Wilson was struggling with drug addiction and depression, his family hired the psychologist to help get him out of his funk. But Landy had some questionable tactics, like moving in with his one and only patient for what he called "twenty-four-hour therapy." What sounds like the kind of concierge therapy for the super rich was actually more of a hostage situation.

Concerned with Landy's tactics, Wilson's family dismissed him after about a year of "treatment," but they hired him again in the early '80s. This time, Landy basically installed himself as Wilson's ill-meaning bestie and took control of his life, executive-producing his music, ghostwriting his autobiography (in which he praised Landy), and taking a huge cut of his songwriting royalties. And that's when he wasn't padlocking the fridge and dousing Wilson with cold water to wake him up in the morning. You know, totally normal therapist stuff. Somehow, Landy even made it into the will. In return for these "services," Landy charged $35,000 per month. After a little over a decade of what the California Board of Medical Quality Assurance realized was a long con, Landy was forced to surrender his license and stay far, far away from Wilson. (It's always so sad when friends grow apart.)

Re: Eternal Damnation

Authorities really didn't have to look any further than Landy and Wilson's never-released rap song, "Smart Girls," for proof of abuse. Landy will have to listen to that abomination for the rest of his afterlife.

—Satan

JEFFREY EPSTEIN

★★★★★
for Playing the Game

> "MAYBE THE ONLY THING WORSE THAN BEING CALLED A PEDOPHILE IS BEING CALLED A HEDGE FUND MANAGER."
>
> —JEFFREY EPSTEIN, PRAGMATIST

No list of Hell-dwelling people would be complete without the more recently departed Jeffrey Epstein. His is a good, old-fashioned American success story about a guy with a dream and a can-do spirit. Unfortunately, that dream was to traumatize girls who weren't old enough to drive by trafficking them to gross old men.

A young Epstein had been teaching math at a private high school in the mid-1970s when a student's father hooked him up with a job at a powerful Wall Street brokerage. (Ah, the good ol' boy network.) Epstein quickly made partner and then started his own firm, building a portfolio worth $1 billion. And the rest is ultra-wealthy white-guy history.

Epstein used his fortune to buy huge mansions and even a private island where he'd entertain his famous friends and clients like Bill Clinton, Prince Andrew, and Donald Trump. In 2005, he was arrested for soliciting a minor—the tip of a child-porn iceberg that could have landed him jail for life—but his high-powered lawyers got him a plea deal, and he kept the pedophile-loaded gravy train rolling. By 2019, the Feds had a solid case against him for sex trafficking minors. Prosecutors were all set to name names at trial when Epstein died by suicide in his prison cell . . . in one of the most surveilled facilities in the country . . . during an uncharacteristic camera outage. That tracks!

Re: Eternal Damnation

Oh, he doesn't want to manage hedge funds? How about doing taxes for the elderly instead? But I have to warn you, Jeff—those older women can get pretty handsy!

—Satan

LOU PEARLMAN

★ ★ ★ ★ ★
for Unmitigated Greed

Florida catches a lot of flak for being home to the weirdest, wildest, and most cringeworthy behavior from humans and animals alike. So it's no wonder that the state was home to most of the boy-band boom of the 1990s. But no one goes to Hell for frosted tips and awkward dance moves. That fate is reserved for managers like Lou Pearlman, who bet big on the boys' naivete and kept the winnings for himself.

Pearlman got his feet wet in the criminal word with a little insurance fraud in the 1980s, insuring a lemon of a blimp for $3 million. Then he used that money to build bands like Backstreet Boys and NSYNC. If Big Poppa (yes, that's what he called himself) had just stopped there, he might have redeemed himself for his earlier criminal enterprises. But enough was never enough for Pearlman (in terms of money, fame, *and* cheeseburgers, by the looks of him). He not only skimmed millions off his golden geese, he also traded on their success to create a Ponzi scheme centered around several fake businesses. Adding insult to injury were rumors from some of his other musical protégés that Pearlman's predatory behavior extended further than their bank accounts. Thankfully, all the schemes and cheeseburgers caught up with him in the end, and he died from heart problems in prison in 2016. So at least that's one less predator for Florida to worry about!

Re: Eternal Damnation

Big Poppa can serve as a flight attendant for private jets and deal with the derision and douchiness of the finance bros who regularly rent them.

—Satan

INDEX